How reassuring is the conclusion?

What view of the world does *A Midsummer Night's Dream* leave us with?

NOTES

Introduction

"Whatever this being of ours is, in its depth and complexity, we see only a little of it, and that little bit is too much for us, incomprehensible."
Mark Doty, *Heaven's Coast*

"We are lived by powers we pretend to understand: They arrange our loves."
W.H. Auden, "In Memory of Ernst Toller"

What explains the special quality of *A Midsummer Night's Dream*? Samuel Johnson called the play "wild and fantastical", noting how "all the parts in their various modes are well written and give the kind of pleasure which the author designed". The 19th-century critic William Hazlitt wrote, in the play's own imagery, of his "wandering in a grove by moonlight" through "a sweetness like odours thrown from beds of flowers". For these critics, the variety of language, character and incident on offer in the *Dream* was particularly pleasant and happy, and suited what they saw as the overall bent of the play towards happiness. G. K. Chesterton responded to "a spirit that unites mankind" in "the mysticism of happiness" and of the play's "pure poetry and intoxication of words", "the amazing artistic and moral beauty" of its design.

One can acknowledge all this, and yet also note how the brightness of that design is full of shadow. Indeed, "shadow" is an important word in the play; the very actors who present it are finally called "shadows". If the play celebrates happiness, it also knows something sadder, not only that unhappiness is possible but that happiness itself may be maintained only by a fragile resolution, perhaps by mere good fortune. Happiness is a kind of gift, perhaps even a kind of grace. In this play, the gift is not withheld, but the play remains very much aware of how it might be, of what slight turn would produce a very different outcome, one not less true to its picture of human life, if less lucky. The end of the comedy banishes what it calls "the blots of Nature's hand", but it knows what and where they are, and that they can all too easily return. Their return, written out in full in other plays, is called tragedy.

THE CHARACTERS

ARISTOCRATS:
Theseus, *Duke of Athens; about to be married to*
Hippolyta, *warrior-queen of the Amazons.*
Egeus, *an old Athenian noble, who wants*
Hermia, *his daughter, to marry*
Demetrius, *a young Athenian noble, rather than*
Lysander, *whom Hermia loves. Her friend,*
Helena, *another Athenian girl, loves Demetrius, who once loved her instead of Hermia.*

CRAFTSMEN:
Peter Quince, *a carpenter, has joined with*
Nick Bottom, *a weaver,*
Tom Snout, *a tinker,*
Robin Starveling, *a tailor,*
Francis Flute, *a bellows-mender, and*
Snug, *a joiner, to rehearse a play in honour of the impending Royal Wedding.*

FAIRIES:
Oberon, *King of the Fairies, attended by*
Puck, *also known as "Robin Goodfellow" and "Hobgoblin", is feuding with*
Titania, *the Fairy Queen, whose fairy attendants include:*
Peaseblosson, Cobweb, Mustardseed and Moth.

A summary of the plot

Theseus, Duke of Athens, has defeated in battle
Hippolyta, Queen of the Amazons, a nation of
warrior women, and the pair are to be married.
They must wait for the new moon for the ceremony
to take place. Interrupting the preparations,
Egeus, a nobleman, brings a complaint against
his daughter, Hermia, for refusing to marry
Demetrius, his chosen spouse, and instead
preferring Lysander. Egeus demands that Hermia
be forced to marry Demetrius or else executed.
Theseus confirms this penalty, adding the option of
lifelong celibacy as a nun, and gives Hermia until
the new moon to decide. Left alone, Lysander and
Hermia decide to elope to his aunt's house, beyond
Athenian jurisdiction. They make arrangements
to meet in the wood outside the city that night, and
tell their plan to Hermia's close friend, Helena,
unrequited in her own love for Demetrius, to
reassure her that the path to her love will now be
clear. Helena, pitifully lamenting her lovelorn
state, decides to betray their plan to Demetrius.

Meanwhile, a group of local craftsmen led by
Peter Quince is planning a play to celebrate the
Royal Wedding. They meet to distribute parts, and
Nick Bottom, a weaver, displays his talents as an
actor. They plan to rehearse secretly at night in
the wood.

Act Two

Night. Puck, the famous Hobgoblin, meets some fairies in the wood and explains to them that a great quarrel has erupted between King Oberon and Queen Titania of Fairyland over possession of a boy Titania has stolen from an Indian King in memory of the boy's dead mother. In consequence of their quarrel, the natural order of the seasons has gone awry. Titania and Oberon meet; she refuses to relinquish the boy, and leaves. In vengeful rage, Oberon commands Puck to fetch a magical flower whose juice laid on the eyes will cause a sleeper to fall in love with the first creature seen on waking. With this he plans to force Titania to give up her Indian boy. While Puck is on his errand, Oberon witnesses Helena in the wood pleading for love with Demetrius, who rejects her. Oberon decides to help Helena and gives Puck some of the flower with instructions to use it on Demetrius.

Titania is sung asleep in the forest by her fairies, and Oberon secretly anoints her eyes with the magical flower.

Lysander and Hermia, tired and lost in the wood, go to sleep until day. Puck finds them and, mistaking Lysander for Demetrius, anoints his eyes with the flower. When Helena appears and awakens him, he immediately falls in love with and woos her. Convinced he is making fun of her, Helena leaves, and Lysander follows. Hermia wakes from a nightmare to find Lysander gone and leaves to find him, fearing the worst.

Act Three

Quince, Bottom and company meet to rehearse
their play, a love tragedy of Pyramus and Thisbe.
They dispute points of staging, but are confounded
and scatter when Bottom reappears with the
head of an ass, transformed by mischievous Puck.
Undaunted, Bottom sings a song, waking Titania,
who falls in love with him and takes him away.

Oberon is delighted to hear of Titania's new
love, but perturbed to observe Hermia accusing
Demetrius of killing Lysander. When Hermia
leaves and Demetrius falls asleep, Oberon sends
Puck to fetch Helena and anoints Demetrius's
eyes. Helena appears, followed by Lysander,
and Demetrius awakes to fall in love with her.
Lysander and Demetrius dispute who has
more claim on Helena, and the three are joined
by Hermia, who accuses Helena of stealing
Lysander's love. Helena accuses all three of
making fun of her, and is especially bitter at
Hermia for betraying her friendship. Demetrius
and Lysander withdraw to duel and the women
part in anger. Puck rounds up all four exhausted
lovers and they fall asleep. Oberon disenchants
Lysander, leaving Demetrius in love with Helena.

Act Four

Titania entertains Bottom in her bower, then falls

asleep with him. Oberon appears and releases her from the spell, since she has now given him the Indian boy. Awaking, she is disgusted with Bottom and leaves with Oberon, requesting explanations.

Theseus and Hippolyta, out hunting, stumble upon the four lovers and wake them. The couples are amazed at the events of the night, and the rearrangement of Demetrius's affections. They consider it a wondrous dream. Theseus, noting the happy outcome, over-rules Egeus's objections so that all three couples can marry together.

Bottom awakes and recalls his night with Titania as "a most rare dream". He returns to his fellow actors, who prepare for their performance before the Duke.

Act Five

Theseus and Hippolyta discuss the lovers' strange story, then all three couples watch and comment on the dreadful performance of "Pyramus and Thisbe", which ends in a country dance. All adjourn to bed, and the Fairy King and Queen lead the fairies in a ceremony of blessing for the newly married couples, promising happiness and perfect children. Puck then sweeps the floor and bids farewell to the audience.

What is *A Midsummer Night's Dream* about?

All Shakespeare's comedies revolve around love, as did those of his contemporaries. Shakespeare would have been familiar with the Latin comedies of Plautus and Terence, Roman playwrights of the second century BC, as these were standard books for boys at the grammar school in Stratford-upon-Avon we are fairly sure he attended. These plays usually feature young lovers, often opposed by old authority, who want to get married, and their plots consist of complicating and then undoing the obstacles they face. Shakespeare, like his contemporaries, tends to follow this pattern.

What is striking about *A Midsummer Night's Dream* is the extent to which love, as well as driving the plot, is a subject of discussion. The characters' experience of love, their journey into or out of it, its effect on their image of themselves and others – all these are central concerns. As Frank Kermode says, the play's "patterns of sight and blindness, wood and city, phantasma and vision, grow into a large and complex statement... of love, vulgar and celestial". Love may not quite make the world go round – but in this play it is crucial to happiness, social order, and even (because the fraying of love between the fairy rulers has disrupted the seasons) the maintenance of good weather.

When, in this first scene, Lysander and Hermia

are lamenting their fate, he speaks of love as

Swift as a shadow, short as any dream,
Brief as the lightning in the collied night,
That, in a spleen, unfolds both heaven and earth,
And ere a man hath power to say 'Behold!'
The jaws of darkness do devour it up:
So quick bright things come to confusion. (1.i)

Lysander's image of love as lightning suggests
its brevity and its power: love is a dangerous
revelation, both fragile and potent. It discloses the
world in a new light, but its glory, like life itself,
can be sadly short. Shortly afterwards, Helena
tries to explain to herself why Demetrius now
loves Hermia where previously he had loved her,
though objective observers can see no difference
("through Athens I am thought as fair as she"). She
thinks out loud:

Things base and vile, holding no quantity,
Love can transpose to form and dignity,
Love looks not with the eyes, but with the mind,
And therefore is winged Cupid painted blind;
Nor has love's mind of any judgment taste. (I.i)

Using the well-known image of Cupid as a
blind boy shooting arrows, Helena is trying to
understand love's irrationality, since she can see
no reason why Demetrius should prefer Hermia

to her. Demetrius "errs", she says, "doting on Hermia's eyes", while she knows that she herself – in thrall to her unreciprocated love for Demetrius – errs in "admiring his qualities". So what is it that causes this irrational love? What is it that makes us "fall" in love in the first place, and why do we fall for one person rather than another?

The distinguished critic Terry Eagleton provides a useful perspective on this:

> If I am in love with you, I must be prepared to explain what it is about you I find so loveable, otherwise the word "love" here has no more meaning than a grunt. I must supply reasons for my affection. But I am also bound to acknowledge that someone else might wholeheartedly endorse my reasons yet not be in love with you at all. The evidence by itself will not decide the issue. At some point along the line, a particular way of seeing the evidence emerges, one which involves a peculiar kind of personal engagement with it; and none of this is reducible to the facts themselves.

What Eagleton calls a "particular way of seeing the evidence" – that is Shakespeare's principal preoccupation in the *Dream*. It is a play about the role of the imagination, and the imagination is what Helena means when she talks of the "mind". "Love looks not with the eyes, but with the mind," she says, but it is the eyes (mentioned more in this play than in any other of Shakespeare's) that give the mind its initial impression, and the first brief assessment of appearance which frequently triggers the imaginative response we call love. love "adds a precious seeing to the eye," insists Berowne in *Love's Labour's Lost*.

> *Tell me where is fancy bred,*
> *Or in the heart or in the head?*
> *How begot, how nourished?*
> *Reply, reply.*
> *It is engender'd in the eyes...*

warns the song in *The Merchant of Venice* as Bassanio surveys the caskets. "Fancy" here, as the critic Stephen Fender notes, "is a delusory view of the whole person": it is the product of what in medieval terminology was known as "ymagynatyf", the mind's power to picture what is not actually before the eyes.

Pretty much from the beginning, Shakespeare was fascinated, and very profoundly so in *A Midsummer Night's Dream*, by the role of the "ymagynatyf" in love, by the conflict – or rift – between it and what Theseus calls "cools reason", between fancy and judgement. Earlier, medieval literature tended to take a Theseus-like, disparaging view of the "ymagynatyf".

Opposite: Judi Dench as Titania in Peter Hall's 1967 film

Medievalists, as Fender says in his valuable study of the *Dream* published in 1968, thought "blind" love was "bad", their "distinctly perjorative attitude" stemming "from a tradition of medieval iconography which associated blindness with evil, with spiritual and physical death".

Shakespeare takes a more different approach. *A Midsummer Night's Dream* does not suggest that blind love is necessarily "bad". Helena's moral lesson on Cupid is, says Fender,

> set in a context that gives it a possible "good" meaning too... The fact that love can change the ugly into the beautiful can be condemned or admired, according to one's point of view. Looked at in one way, it is obviously absurd, and Theseus makes it an occasion for satire... But from another point of view it can be seen as an act of almost divine creativity.

Cool reason, in the play's terms, has its limits; it provides much less than the imagination of whatever makes life worth living; the imagination, through dreams and art as well as through love, can transform the world for us.

Theseus himself is far from immune: he lectures his Amazon bride-to-be on wishful (romantic) thinking but, as Graham Bradshaw observes in *Shakespeare's Scepticism*, he is a lover too, so places himself in a "comically false position" when he tells his bride what lovers, lunatics and poets have in common. He cannot see that his own speech denouncing lovers and the imagination in Act Five is itself a miracle of the creative imagination. Indeed, as has been pointed out, the whole play can be seen as an ironic refutation of his thesis that the imagination is to be despised. In this Theseus, not Bottom, is the real "ass" of the *Dream*. Bradshaw writes:

> Theseus's rationalism is itself irrational... His refusal to submit his blinkered dogmatic scepticism to a radically sceptical self-scrutiny is associated with a larger denial of those life-mysteries to which he is himself subject – mysteries which may be apprehended, but not comprehended.

A Midsummer Night's Dream, says Marjorie Garber, "is throughout a celebration of the irrationality of love, not a criticism of the failure of reason".

Indeed what is thought of as reason is often no such thing. Recent critics like Louis Montrose and Shirley Nelson Garner have drawn attention to the way the idea of reason in the play is always shadowed by the question: "who decides what is reasonable"? What Theseus and Oberon really care about, and want, is not reason but power, and the real conflict in the play is not so much between love and reason as between love and power. From the first conversation in the opening scene, when Theseus discusses his forthcoming wedding with Hippolyta, the demands of love in the *Dream* are entangled with the demands of authority. Theseus, who reminds Hippolyta, perhaps tactlessly, that

SHAKESPEARE'S HEAVY FATHERS

In his study of the *Dream*, the critic James Calderwood takes a Freudian view of Egeus's attempt to choose a son-in-law. "Giving away a daughter in marriage," he says, "can be a kind of belated castration for a father." It is a painful parting, "only slightly anaesthetized by the pleasurable opportunity to engage in one final piece of tyranny, choosing the right husband himself." Like other "heavy fathers" in Shakespeare, Egeus's real concern is not to choose a husband for his daughter but a son-in-law for himself. "Since these sons-in-law are so uniformly distasteful to the daughters, we might suspect that they are chosen at least partly as a vindictive consolation for the father's own loss." Lysander even taunts Demetrius by saying: "You have her father's love, Demetrius;/ Let me have Hermia's."

But as Juliet, Jessica in *The Merchant of Venice* and Hermia all rebelliously demonstrate, Shakespeare's daughters are not always prepared to be handed over to sons-in-law chosen for them; they want to do the choosing themselves. Even the otherwise pliant Miranda in *The Tempest* disobeys her father's command not to speak to Ferdinand, though her father, Prospero, secretly approves of their love ■

he "wooed thee with my sword", and that their wedding is the result of military conquest, has a heroic history made up less of "cool reason" than hot reason, or just plain force. Then Egeus comes barrelling in with his complaint that his daughter Hermia won't marry Demetrius, and she defies him.

HERMIA:

> *I would my father looked but with my eyes*

THESEUS:

> *Rather your eyes must with his judgement look. (I.i)*

Hermia must choose one of two men. Is she being unreasonable in choosing the *wrong* one? Lest we are tempted to side with Egeus, Shakespeare quickly gives the other side a voice. Lysander says he will make just as good a husband as Demetrius ("I am... as well derived as he... My fortunes every way as fairly ranked...") and moreover, he says, Hermia loves him: "Why should not I then prosecute my right?" Why indeed. Egeus accuses Lysander of the theft of Hermia's imagination; he rages that the young man has "stolen the impression of her fantasy", replacing her father's authority with his own. Egeus may be right, but what he really wants is the power to choose his own son-in-law, and far from seeming reasonable, his rage is just as irrational as his daughter's love, and Theseus's decision to back him seems so too.

But while the *Dream* is sympathetic to the imagination as the source of much that is worthwhile in life, it neither disguises nor minimises the dangers of irrational love. Imagination gives us the capacity to abandon what we know and what we have been, and to become something different, which makes us more interesting, more vital, more dynamic. It *does* link love, art and lunacy, as Theseus suggests (one might add dreaming too), though not on his terms. In making this plain, the play encourages us to wonder about *all* acts of valuing. "We are brought to ask," says Bradshaw, "how many of those things large or small which 'give' life value – including love and friendship, and the liking for dogs, hunting or plays – depend on that shaping fantasy."

At the same time, our imaginations, in putting us at risk from shaping fantasies, also make us vulnerable to powers that may not value our vitality, that may merely wish us harm, or wish us to be *theirs*. We are made aware throughout the *Dream* of how easily things can go wrong. The playlet which the "mechanicals" rehearse and then perform in the final act is an ironic reminder of this. In it we also hear of a father who harshly opposes the marriage of his daughter, but here, as Marjorie Garber says, "the result is not reconciliation, but tragic death for the lovers. Similarly, the menacing forest of the playlet, which contains the fatal lion, stands as a tragic alternative to the amiable world of the Athenian wood..." The playlet thus has a "cathartic" effect. It "absorbs and disarms the tragic alternative, the events which did not happen. Art becomes a way of containing and triumphing over unbearable reality."

A Midsummer Night's Dream sees the imagination as both liberating and enslaving. It can be either or both and, at a deeper level, this contradictoriness implies a radical view of the coherence of human personality. The *Dream*, like much of Shakespeare's work, challenges the very idea that anyone has, or is, a single, stable self. In truth we are inhabited by many possible selves, some of which we can barely recognise or acknowledge, some of which beckon to our innermost desires, some of which are forced on us willy-nilly. As Hermia says to Theseus, "I know not by what power I am made bold," and Demetrius later observes: "I wot [know] not by what power/ – But by some power it is – my love to Hermia/ Melted as the snow." With an almost magical quickness, we may become unrecognisable to our (old) selves and to others, our supposedly rational self-awareness deformed by wilfulness both our own and not our own, as though we were only dreaming ourselves all along.

What are we supposed to make of Theseus?

Both Theseus and Hippolyta, his intended bride, would have been known to those in Shakespeare's audience who were versed in the classics. He is "Duke Theseus" here (as he was in Chaucer's

THE LIFE AND TIMES OF THESEUS

Shakespeare learned about Theseus from a variety of sources, including Plutarch, Ovid and Chaucer. Here are some of the incidents central to the legend.

1 As a young man, he travelled to Athens to meet his estranged father, Aegeus, killing a series of monsters and criminals along the way and making the land route safe for later travellers. On the journey, he also raped Perigenia, the daughter of one of his victims.

2 From Athens, he sailed to Crete to rescue the Athenians from Cretan persecution by killing the Minotaur, a bull-headed man-monster kept in a labyrinth under King Minos's palace.

3 In Crete, he was assisted by the King's daughter, Ariadne, who gave him a ball of thread to guide his return from the labyrinth. He fled Crete with Ariadne, but abandoned her on the island of Naxos during his return voyage.

4 His war with the Amazons began when he abducted their queen – either

"Knight's Tale" from which Shakespeare took part of his story), but he is also the famous Greek hero, slayer of the Minotaur and ruler of Athens. Views of him were traditionally positive, and throughout the play he is given speeches that endorse him as a hero of both physical and moral gifts. The play draws on his association with other

Hippolyta or Antiopa, according to different accounts.

5 He was the legendary ruler and great mythical lawgiver of Athens in the cycle of Greek myths.

6 His marriage to Hippolyta resulted in one child, a boy named Hippolytus. Theseus's later wife, Phaedra, fell in love with Hippolytus as a young man. When he rejected her, she told Theseus he had tried to rape her. Theseus asked the god Poseidon to avenge him, and Hippolytus was dragged to death by his own horses, terrified by a sea-monster.

7 He was a friend of Hercules, who later released him from the underworld, where he was imprisoned after attempting to abduct Queen Persephone for his best friend, Pirithous.

8 While attending the wedding banquet of Pirithous, he became involved in a drunken brawl with centaurs attending the feast, killing many of them.

9 In 475 BC, the Athenian general Cimon claimed to have found Theseus's bones on the island of Scyros, where he was believed to have been murdered after losing power, and returned them to Athens for burial ■

founder-heroes of the ancient classical world, such as Hercules and Cadmus. Like those two, goes the myth, Theseus brought human order to an unruly wilderness full of criminals and monsters. Renaissance commentators shared this view. The translation of Ovid's great Latin poem *Metamorphoses* described the deeds of Theseus as "a spur to prowess and a glass [that is, a mirror showing] / How princes' sons and noblemen their youthful years should pass". To invoke the name of Theseus in the Renaissance is to invoke the very image of a rational heroic ruler.

Earlier critics endorsed this positive view of Theseus. G. Wilson Knight saw him as "the calmest and wisest [of men]" who "shows an exquisite and wide love and deep human knowledge" and "can smile at the extravagances of undisciplined fancy" since he "holds the balance exact of earthliness and spirituality". G.K. Chesterton said he was "the incarnation of a happy and generous rationalism", and Ernest Schanzer likewise called him "balanced and rational". Paul Olson, another critic from the 1950s, went further, naming him, approvingly, the "King of Order".

But, as we have already noted, there are difficulties with this view. An obvious one is that Theseus's first action in the play is hardly consistent with what we think of as reason. Appealed to by Egeus to judge between himself and his daughter, Theseus does not hesitate.

He insists to Hermia that "to you your father should be as a god" and that her "eyes must with his judgment look" according to the Law of Athens, "which by no means we may extenuate". Blind adherence to a death-dealing and coercive law is hardly the hallmark of rational rule, no matter how much Theseus attempts to disguise it in reasonable language. Critics who endorse Theseus's judgement here tend to patronise Hermia and trivialise the threat she faces. Stuart Tave, another critic fond of Theseus ("a very sensible man and a good ruler"), calls her "a rather naughty little girl". And Tony Tanner, speaking of the follies of the younger mortals in the play, says we are to contrast them with "the sane and steady love of the mature figures, Theseus and Hippolyta". It's an odd line to take since the love between Theseus and Hippolyta has not been at all steady, and has its origins in a very *un*steady place.

For all the talk of Theseus as a prudent rationalist, it's important to recall that the hero also had his darker side in classical myth – as did his "kinsman Hercules", who once murdered his entire family in a fit of madness inflicted by a vengeful goddess. Theseus was notorious as a serial seducer and abandoner of women, and the play is careful to remind us of this directly when Oberon accuses Titania of having helped the Duke in these very exploits:

Didst thou not lead him through the glimmering
                                    night
From Perigenia, whom he ravishèd?
And make him with fair Aegle break his faith,
With Ariadne and Antiopa? (II.i)

Shakespeare didn't have to include these sordid
details, but he does. And while Titania calls
the accusation of her assistance "the forgeries
of jealousy", she doesn't attempt to deny that
Theseus did these things. And at the end of his
career, he rashly asked the god Poseidon to kill his
son, Hippolytus, after a later wife, Phaedra, falsely
accused the youth of attempted rape. So, no matter
how reasonable he appears in Shakespeare's
play, his history outside of it is a decidedly mixed
one. Hippolyta's name might even be expected to
remind those who knew their myths of this later,
tragic hastiness.

Hippolyta, the bride Shakespeare gives him,
was among Theseus's earlier conquests – literally
so, as one of his great deeds was defeating in battle
the all-female army of the Amazons led by her.
The play opens with him impatiently expecting
their wedding "in another key/ With pomp, with
triumph and with reveling". Triumph is a rather
tactless word, since it originally meant a victory
procession leading captive enemies. A.D. Nuttall,
among others, has objected to this aspect of
Theseus, calling him "a sexual bully" who "can't

stop strutting" and who "is characterised from the beginning as owning a sort of insensitivity that is perhaps peculiar to males". If nothing else, his rejection of the imagination as the province of "the lunatic, the lover and the poet" is undercut by the fact that he is himself an ancient and powerful poetic fable, the product not of "cool reason" but of "strong imagination".

This is just one of what Graham Bradshaw calls the "sly ironies, large and small" which "point to the place of the irrational in Theseus's own life". We may see in the distance between these more recent critical views and the earlier ones how sceptical about rational rulers, especially male ones, criticism has become in recent decades.

So Theseus has backgrounds of both heroism and sexual crime, both reason and unreason, and while the former may be more prominent in Shakespeare's play the latter is by no means absent. The way Theseus is presented is much more ambiguous than most critics allow. And in all that follows his first appearance, it is love's *un*reason – its violence, which is Shakespeare's primary concern.

The whole play can be seen as built round the Theseus legend. Even his most famous exploit – the killing of the Minotaur in the Cretan labyrinth – is echoed in the memorable stage image at the centre of the play: the Fairy Queen's love for the mortal with an ass's head. The play may not be a dream *of* Theseus, as some productions have suggested, but it might fairly be described as a dream, or at least a poetic fantasy, *about* him and the implications of his history, in all their contradictions. As the critic Norman Holland has put it: "Throughout the play, the ruler, the father, the lovers, the King of the Fairies, the amateur actors, and even the audience at the play within the play – all proclaim love, but they also threaten violence or humiliation." That dichotomy is present from the start, and even before the start, in the selection of Theseus as the play's presiding human.

How much does Shakespeare owe to Ovid?

An interviewer once asked the French philosopher, Jacques Derrida, whether he had actually read the multitude of books on the shelves in his office. "Not at all," Derrida replied, "I have only ever read four books!"* He was making a point about what he considered *real* reading to be – an intense commitment to understanding someone else's work to which one returns again and again. Such reading is really a kind of ongoing dialogue, even an argument, between reader and

*Sadly, we don't know which they were.

book. Many people have read Shakespeare's plays in this way, and it is clear from his work that he too read some particular books like this, and used them to feed and shape his own writing.

One of the books that Shakespeare really *read* was Ovid's great poem, the *Metamorphoses*. The poem is based on a series of myths of classical antiquity in which the powerful emotions felt by gods and humans – love, lust, rage, envy, pride, fear, despair – lead to humans being transformed into animals, birds and even plants. Gods, being stronger than mortals, survive unchanged; but for the mortals, Ovid's world is one of strange shape-shifting magic and terrible outbursts: sudden, unpredictable, and above all dangerous. A few of his stories are still well-known: Narcissus falling in love with his reflection, for example, or Adonis being loved by Venus and killed by a wild boar. In Shakespeare's time, these stories offered a vivid and intense world outside the Christian tradition on which writers could draw to display their learning, or embellish their work, or explore philosophical and moral questions.

Shakespeare uses Ovid's poem in all these ways, but also for a deeper purpose. Ovid seems to have provided him with a way of seeing the world – or at least strengthened the way in which he already saw it. *Metamorphoses*, as its title suggests, is about *change*, not just in bodies but in minds and souls too. Terrible emotions take hold of Ovid's characters and utterly remake their sense of the world, forcing them to do things – often disastrous ones – they would never have imagined doing before. Ovid's poem is about extremity, about the limits of what can be felt and endured by human beings, about the point where everyday ideas and emotions are heightened or twisted into strangeness. Jonathan Bate is right to call

OVID
_____

Publius Ovidius Naso, known in English as Ovid, has been for ten centuries the most influential poet in Western art. He was born in 43 BC in the town of Sulmo, now Sulmona, some 75 miles east across the Apennines from Rome. His father's family were established provincial gentry, and sent him to Rome in his teens for instruction by famous tutors in rhetoric, the normal prelude to magisterial office and membership in the Senate.

But Ovid had other ideas. As a young and ambitious provincial writer, he cultivated literary circles in the great metropolis. By day he was a student and, later, a minor magistrate; by night and in his leisure time, he was a poet and a reveller in the urban world. Soon he declined further official advancement and withdrew into the private life of a poet. From early bravura performances in the "Amores" and "Heroides", to his unfinished poem on the religious calendar of Rome, "Fasti", Ovid was

Ovid "rational Rome's great counter-visionary, its magical thinker". Change, for Ovid, is not merely evident in the world, it is a condition of belonging to it, an inevitable part of being alive.

Along with his particular stories, Shakespeare took from Ovid this sense of the way we are all exposed to change, both in ourselves and in everyone and everything around us. This idea

spectacularly successful in his chosen career.

Rather too much so, in fact. His erotic verse, playfully extolling love affairs and adultery, eventually drew the ire of a moralising emperor, and in 8 AD Augustus banished Ovid, the libertine poet and self-proclaimed trumpeter of his own vices, to the small town of Tomis on the Black Sea, the far border of the Roman world. Although he wrote a series of begging verse letters back to Rome, neither his friends nor his poems moved Augustus, or Tiberius his successor. Ovid lived on in cold Tomis, drnking frozen wine, and died there ten years later at the age of 60, far from his wife and the city he loved.

Metamorphoses, the poem for which he is now best known, is an epic in 15 books, charting the history of the world from Creation to the death of Julius Caesar. It is most famous as a compilation and retelling of major Greek and Roman myths, and is the major source for many famous tales, such as those of Narcissus, Adonis, Pygmalion, Arachne, Actaeon, Perseus and others. In addition to its intrinsic poetic interest, it has served as an immense quarry for later artists to borrow from and adapt, as Shakespeare did throughout his career, and especially in *A Midsummer Night's Dream* ■

runs through *A Midsummer Night's Dream.* Even the regular changes of the seasons cannot be relied on; think of Titania's great speech about the scrambled weather in which "thorough this distemperature we see the seasons alter". "Hoary headed-frosts fall in the fresh lap of the crimson rose," she says: old and young, early and late, heads and laps, are all mixed up, so that "The mazèd world now knows not which is which".

The phrase reflects Shakespeare's view of nature: not only are humans "amazed" by the strange changes of the world, but the world itself threatens to turn into a maze, in which they get lost on ever-branching paths. The wood in which most of the action occurs is just such a "mazèd" place; the word "wood" is also an old term for "mad". As Demetrius complains when lost in it, one can all too easily go "wood within the wood".

In the way characters in the *Dream* find themselves changing in themselves and in their feelings for others, Shakespeare is responding to the aspect of Ovid which led Camille Paglia to call him "the first psychoanalyst of sex". For Ovid, as for Shakespeare, says Paglia, "identity is liquid". The imagination that shapes and governs our

Opposite: Calista Flockhart as Helena in the 1999 film directed by Michael Hoffman. Titania was played by Michelle Pfeiffer, Demetrius by Christian Bale, and Lysander by Dominic West.

desires mutates – and it has a strange will of its own, often regardless of what we might choose or want. So we fall in love with the wrong people, we change ourselves to fit them, or try to, and they too change and elude our grasp.

In Ovid's poem, these sudden inscrutable feelings are so strong that they can change actual bodies. In Shakespeare's play, the kind of literal body-transformation so frequent in Ovid is confined to the joke that Puck plays on Bottom when he gives Bottom an ass's head in place of his human one. But metaphorical shape-shifting occurs elsewhere. Helena describes herself in her love-torments as Demetrius's "spaniel", and imagines her pursuit of him as part of a topsy-turvy world in which her love for Demetrius has turned both of them into wild beasts:

DEMETRIUS:
> *I'll run from thee and hide me in the brakes,*
> *And leave thee to the mercy of wild beasts.*

HELENA:
> *The wildest hath not such a heart as you.*
> *Run when you will, the story shall be changed:*
> *Apollo flies, and Daphne holds the chase;*
> *The dove pursues the griffin, the mild hind*
> *Makes speed to catch the tiger. (II.i)*

Ovid's presence here is obvious from the reference to Apollo and Daphne, one of the Roman poet's most famous tales.*

A more complex example occurs when Lysander speaks of his elopement with Hermia as planned for "To-morrow night, when Phoebe doth behold/ Her silver visage in the watery glass". Lysander pictures the moon as the classical goddess, Phoebe (Apollo's sister), looking at herself in the mirroring surface of a pond. Her posture echoes Ovid's tale of Narcissus, who fell in love with his own reflection in a pond. But the echo of Narcissus isn't just decorative. It suggests how falling in love changes the way we think about *ourselves*, as well as about those with whom we fall in love. All through the play, as Marjorie Garber points out, the characters face the question of what the familiar world has been transformed into, and what they themselves have suddenly become. "Am I not Hermia? Are you not Lysander?" asks Hermia in the wood and, Garber comments,

> this is a question that will be asked, in various modes and keys, by Bottom and Titania and by

* In Book One of the *Metamorphoses,* Cupid takes revenge on Apollo for taunting him by shooting him with an arrow of desire, causing him to love Daphne, a nymph who has been shot with the contrary leaden arrow of disdain. Apollo furiously chases Daphne, crying out that though "lambs flee from wolves and hinds from lions, and the fluttering doves from eagles" he is not someone to flee from. But just as he is about to catch her, Daphne prays to her river-god father and is changed into a laurel tree, evading Apollo, who instead makes her his symbolic tree.

Helena and Demetrius, as the world of the Athenian wood strips them of what they thought were their identities.

Thus, while Hermia seems quite happy with herself as Lysander's lover, Helena's self-image undergoes a terrible debasement for love:

> *I am as ugly as a bear,*
> *For beasts that meet me run away for fear,*
> *Therefore no marvel though Demetrius do. (II.ii)*

Such imagined transformations are everywhere. When Oberon envisages Titania as in love with "lion, bear or wolf or bull/ Or meddling monkey or busy ape", his malicious fantasies remind us of Ovid's world of mutable bodies – as does Puck who, in addition to doling out all this change through the magic flower, is also appropriately a shape-shifter:

> *Sometime a horse I'll be, sometime a hound,*
> *A hog, a headless bear, sometime a fire. (III.i)*

Puck boasts of appearing as a three-legged stool or a roasted crab-apple in a drink, or "neighing in likeness of a filly-foal". He can be anywhere and anything, a veritable image of the malleable shifting and unreliable world, an Ovidian imp. And as if he is acknowledging where all this mutability comes from, Shakespeare takes directly from Ovid's poem the tale of "Pyramus and Thisbe" which the workmen stage in Act Five. Frank Kermode, indeed, has even called the *Dream* "a set of variations on the theme of Pyramus and Thisbe".

All Shakespeare's love stories show the way our lives and selves can be overthrown by a sudden surge of transformative emotion: Romeo catapulted out of his Montague world by meeting Juliet, or Othello abandoning his lifelong soldier's solitude for Desdemona's love. Reading Ovid provided Shakespeare with a fund of powerful images for such change, images which enable us to see his characters more vividly, and to realise what's at stake for them. In the wood, the young lovers must come to terms with forces they never knew existed, or existed in such deforming potency. These large, inhuman or dehumanising forces are symbolised for Ovid in the literal deforming changes that his bodies undergo. Shakespeare draws on this. He draws, too, on the dramatic powers of magic to show the sudden, wrenching changes which love can produce.

Why is magic so important in the play?

A Midsummer Night's Dream is very interested in how much of what happens to us in life happens without our consent. We are only ever partly "ourselves", Shakespeare suggests, and subject to powers and manipulations that little care for our conscious desires. The use of magic in the play is a vivid way of showing this: characters who have a spell put on them do not act by their own choice, even if they think they do; their passions are arbitrary and compelled. Magic has no interest in the nature of its victims; it transforms us whether we like it or not.

The fairy magic in the play stages directly this sense that much of our experience, especially our experience of love, comes from causes that we have no control of, and that have no relation to or interest in who we are. As far as the fairies are concerned, all mortals are more or less alike. Indeed the mortal lovers in the forest are practically indistinguishable. Puck has no interest in which is which and blithely mistakes Demetrius for Lysander. Like the love-juice itself, he does not discriminate.

Shakespeare's characterisation of the lovers follows the logic of love and fairy-magic. Critics have noted how hard it is to distinguish the two men from one another, or the two women. "Shakespeare wants to show that whatever individuality people may cherish in themselves, certain basic impulses can make them behave very like other people," says Stephen Fender. "Presenting his characters as devoid of individual personalities is a useful way of translating this thematic statement into dramatic terms." The men in particular seem distinguishable only because the women, being in love with them, can tell them apart. Lysander even makes this point himself when he compares his qualities with Demetrius's:

> *I am, my lord, as well derived as he,*
> *As well possess'd; my love is more than his;*
> *My fortunes every way as fairly rank'd,*
> *If not with vantage, as Demetrius';*
> *And, which is more than all these boasts can be,*
> *I am beloved of beauteous Hermia. (I.i)*

The *only* difference Lysander can cite between them is the quite contingent fact that Hermia loves him. As for the women: they are more differentiated than the men, as Harold Brooks points out in his introduction to the Arden *Dream*. Helena is tall and fair, Hermia short and dark; "Hermia is spirited and warm-blooded, tender in happy love, hot and militant in anger. Helena is much more the lady: very feminine, and very much aware of it." But these differences never seem very important. Helena insists in various ways that she and Hermia are equals, except for the fact that she is *not* loved: "Through Athens I am thought as fair as she,/ But what of that: Demetrius thinks not so." And when she wishes to appeal to her "ancient love" for Hermia, her account of it emphasises just how similar they have been:

As if our hands, our sides, voices and minds,

QUEEN ELIZABETH

When *A Midsummer Night's Dream* was first performed, Elizabeth had been Queen for about 35 years. The play was not dedicated to her, nor, as far as we know, commissioned either by her or in her honour. She may never have seen it. Harold Brooks says that "most scholars are agreed that the *Dream* was designed to grace a wedding in a noble household" and "it seems likely that Queen Elizabeth was present". But there is no good, direct evidence for this, and Peter Holland, another editor, disputes Brooks's claim.

The play does contain one clear reference to the Queen. Oberon recalls how he saw flying Cupid take aim "at a fair vestal thronèd by the west" though he also saw how the arrow missed and "the imperial votaress passèd on, In maiden meditation, fancy-free". This imperial virgin is clearly meant as a compliment to Elizabeth, the unmarried queen who had declared that her only

Had been incorporate. So we grew together,
Like to a double cherry, seeming parted,
But yet an union in partition. (III.ii)

Even their names signal this likeness: both have six letters, and both begin and end with the same letters.

The magical causation of love in *Dream* underlines the essential impersonality of erotic

spouse was England.

But critics differ as to whether or not the Queen is implicated more subtly in the play. Jonathan Bate wonders why the compliment was included at all and thinks it "may have been an attempt to forestall a dangerous identification elsewhere". Since Elizabeth had been imagined by the poet Edmund Spenser as "the Faerie Queene" in a recent epic poem with that title, Bate suggests that "by identifying the Queen with the imperial votaress, Shakespeare denies the transgressive identification of her with Titania". That is, the Queen is mentioned in the play in one very obvious place in order that she *not*

be seen in the play in a more dangerous one.

Other critics, such as Louis Montrose, have insisted that the defensive gesture is only a diversion from a deeper connection between the Queen's political mythology and the play's treatment of Titania. For Montrose, the latter is a sly, even unconscious, response to the "pervasive cultural presence" of the Queen. He points out that the Queen's reign provided a strong example close to home of things that the play pushes to the edges of its story: female power, celibacy, sisterhood. Proudly unmarried, proclaiming herself "a prince", rallying excitement – even if it leads, paradoxically, to an intense and intimate attention to the person beloved – and shows that we are all vulnerable to it. To those who wield its power – whether Cupid or Puck – mortals are all the same, foolish members of Puck's "fond pageant".

Puck himself is like a symbol of the arbitrariness of love. His character is evoked by another fairy as

---

her troops for war with Spain, surrounded at court by her ladies-in-waiting, the Queen was a paradox, even an affront, to the traditional rule of men.

Certainly, Elizabeth's presence on the throne in what we now call "the Elizabethan period" is the background of everything going on in the play. But the argument that *A Midsummer Night's Dream* stages a more or less explicit humiliation of the Queen has to confront the fact that the play was successful. The censors of the time, who were quite active, surely couldn't have seen a direct affront to Queen Elizabeth or they would never have

allowed it. Perhaps readers and audiences were less conscious of Elizabeth than modern commentators think they ought to have been. Yet the possibility of offending the monarch may add extra edge to Puck's final worry about whether "we shadows have offended".

In 2010, Dame Judi Dench, in a production directed by Sir Peter Hall, played Queen Elizabeth herself attending a performance of *A Midsummer Night's Dream* and then joining in the action as Titania. One can only imagine what the Virgin Queen, whose motto was *semper eadem* (Latin for "always the same"), would have made of this ∎

That frights the maidens of the villagery;
Skim milk, and sometimes labour in the quern
And bootless make the breathless housewife
churn;
And sometime make the drink to bear no barm;
Mislead night-wanderers, laughing at their
harm. (II.i)

He is an ancient kind of spirit, at home in farm and woodland. He is a shape-shifter, associated with wildfire and swiftness, an unreliable servant, fond of mischief and the unexpected. He has no companions, and though he acts as Oberon's servant his tricks undermine his master's plans and he keeps a certain independence of outlook. Like Ariel in Shakespeare's late play, *The Tempest,* who serves Prospero the magician, and perhaps like Loge, the fire-spirit in Richard Wagner's *Ring* operas, who helps chief god Wotan, he has somewhat vexed relations with his magical boss. Unlike them, he is not set free at the end.

If Puck is an energetic trickster, the fairy monarchs, Oberon and Titania, are more like Renaissance princes, with their duelling prerogatives, their trains of servants and their progresses around the "fairy kingdom". Shakespeare makes the fertility and abundance of nature itself depend on them, as Titania complains in describing the current weather disaster which is

43

the result of their quarrels:

> *And thorough this distemperature we see*
> *The seasons alter: hoary-headed frosts*
> *Fall in the fresh lap of the crimson rose,*
> *And on old Hiems' thin and icy crown*
> *An odorous chaplet of sweet summer buds*
> *Is, as in mockery, set: the spring, the summer,*
> *The childing autumn, angry winter, change*
> *Their wonted liveries, and the mazèd world,*
> *By their increase, now knows not which is which:*
> *And this same progeny of evils comes*
> *From our debate, from our dissension;*
> *We are their parents and original. (II.i)*

Though Oberon and Titania may not be weather gods, the natural world and its cycles in the *Dream* depends on their harmonious amity. They are, as it were, an image of parents seen by the eye of childhood: when they quarrel, the whole world goes to hell. The picture of their relations shows how deeply the play values hierarchy and concord, though it also shows their relationship as fragile and provides a sharp commentary on the imminent marriages. It also echoes, of course, the relationship between Theseus and Hippolyta. In his much praised RSC production of the *Dream* in 1970, Peter Brook underlined this by having the same actor and actress play both roles, a doubling

up which has become common in modern productions. This doubling, says Helen Hackett, contributes to the dream elements of the play's plot because

> it creates a sense that the fairy action... is related to and a reflection of the action in the outer Athenian frame; that Oberon and Titania are the dream-personae of Theseus and Hippolyta through which the Athenian couple can enact their secret desires and work out their buried resentments.

Most of the older, more traditional criticism of the *Dream* defended Oberon's imposition of his will on Titania by using the magic flower as a return to "normal" authority. But this view takes too little note of Oberon's motives. He does not frame his deed as an attempt to restore order but as a gesture of vengeance: "Well, go thy way. Thou shalt not from this grove," he tells the departing Titania, "Till I torment thee for this injury." His main motive as he anoints his sleeping Queen's eyes is very clear:

> *Be it ounce, or cat, or bear,*
> *Pard, or boar with bristled hair*
> *In thine eye that shall appear*
> *When thou wakst, it is thy dear:*
> *Wake when some vile thing is near. (II.ii)*

The last line, added as a stinging afterthought, is hardly the instruction of an enlightened philosopher-king rectifying the balance of nature. Though the play may ultimately appear to confirm the authority of rulers like Oberon and Theseus and the hierarchy they head, it takes care to show how that authority can be motivated by anger and is policed by coercion.

The fairy love-magic in the play is executed through the "little western flower", the violent result of Cupid's arrow going astray from its intended target, an "imperial votaress" who passes on "in maiden meditation, fancy free". The story is a gesture of compliment to Queen Elizabeth for having evaded the snares of desire for so long. But when it swerves aside from the Virgin Queen, the arrow falls on the flower, "before milk-white, now purple with love's wound" and turns it into a potent love-spell. The very landscape of the flower's creation is evocative of the force of love-magic in the play. Oberon sets the scene as he tells Puck:

> *Thou rememberest*
> *Since once I sat upon a promontory,*
> *And heard a mermaid on a dolphin's back*
> *Uttering such dulcet and harmonious breath*
> *That the rude sea grew civil at her song*
> *And certain stars shot madly from their spheres,*
> *To hear the sea-maid's music. (II.i)*

"The sea," as Camille Paglia says, "is the master-image in Shakespeare's plays" and Oberon evokes a profoundly Shakespearean land-and-seascape, all energy and flow. In Shakespeare, Paglia adds:

> Everything is in flux – thought, language, identity, action [in] the huge fateful rhythm which is his plot, an overwhelming force entering the play from beyond society. Shakespeare's elemental energy comes from nature itself.

Sitting on his promontory – itself sticking out into the wild water – Oberon listens to a music that is also full of contrary energies, at once calming the "rude" waters and stirring the silent stars to a kind of erotic frenzy. And the purple flower that Cupid's arrow creates when it misses its intended target suggests both the psychological wound to the self that love causes, and the loss of virginity in sexual action that love may lead to. Both its power and its danger appear clearly in the myth of its origin, just as they are demonstrated in its use in the plot.

But strangely, no sooner is the flower in Oberon's hand than he divides the power it gives him to shape the experience of others. Its splitting between the vengeful Fairy King, the play's active sponsor of sexual hierarchy, and the antithetical anarchic Puck, who freely admits that "those things do best please me/ That befall preposterously", is Shakespeare's way of showing the essential ungovernability of the erotic imagination. Critics who see Oberon as a force for good tend to overlook the power he gives Puck. Oberon's aim may be to enforce his will on his Queen, and to put Helena and Demetrius's relationship back on a "normal" track, but the magic flower is no sooner in Puck's hands than it makes things worse; soon both Demetrius and Lysander are running after Helena and leaving Hermia loverless. Only the casual appearance of a second flower from Oberon's herbal arsenal can stabilise things once more.

Stanley Tucci as Puck and Rupert Everett as Oberon in Michael Hoffman's 1999 film.

But this second, curative herb – "Dian's bud" – is given no explanatory myth in the play; it is really no more than a convenient shorthand for putting things "right". But things – the play implies – will invariably go wrong again. They always do.

The waywardness of "Cupid's flower" reveals the difficulty of reconciling individual imagination with social order. The problem is not just that parents and children may disagree on the choice of partners, as Egeus and Hermia do. It is, more fundamentally, that the very faculty that is supposed to motivate marriage, underpin it and hold it together – the erotic imagination – is altogether unsuited to the purpose. The implication is clear: the goal of Theseus, of Oberon, and, at least in part, of Shakespearean comedy – the goal of making social structure and sexual feeling align in marriage – is not much better than a pipe dream. The ever-changing character of fantasy as a driver of human motive will ensure that such social engineering sooner or later goes awry, as it has done with Oberon and Titania, or with Demetrius's infatuation with Hermia. Though Puck, that spirit of the restless imagination at play, may ultimately resume his place as Oberon's servant, sooner or later he will be off into the wildness again, "swifter than arrow from the Tartar's bow". Terry Eagleton's image of Puck as "the delusive space towards which the hunters in the forest are drawn" underlines this central truth of the play. The lesson of Puck's possession of the flower cannot be exorcised simply by bringing the play to an end for an evening. His anarchic spirit will return. There will always be another dream tomorrow.

Why did Shakespeare bring in the "mechanicals"?

Alongside the worlds of aristocratic Athens and feuding fairies, Shakespeare includes in the *Dream* a group of amateur actors rehearsing a play. The play is the "lamentable comedy and most cruel death of Pyramus and Thisbe" based on a classical story, but Quince, Bottom and Company are recognisably local and English, rather than ancient Athenian, as the names of the actors and the jigging 14-syllable English verses of their playscript tell us. The troupe must have seemed very familiar to early theatre-goers; Shakespeare may have known amateur actors like them, from his native Stratford-upon-Avon or elsewhere. But what are these English countrymen – "rude mechanicals," as Puck calls them – doing in a story about ancient Athens, and why are they rehearsing a play?

The names and professions of the actors provide one clue. They are all "handicraft men", either makers or menders, with names related to their jobs. Quince is a carpenter ("quoins" were wedges); Snug a joiner – another kind of woodworker. Snout is a tinker – a domestic metalworker, Starveling a tailor (tailors were notoriously thin), Flute a bellows-mender, and Bottom a weaver (a "bottom" was a packet of thread). The *making* involved in producing what Peter Quince calls "a play fitted" is underlined by their professional making – of tools, garments, cloth, furniture.

The introduction of these amateur actors by Shakespeare into his own play would have been recognised immediately by Bertolt Brecht, the great German dramatist, as a way of bringing the construction of the play itself into deliberate focus. Brecht would have called it an "alienation effect", that is, a strategy for forcing us to notice how the dramatic event is constructed, rather than merely letting it wash over us. As long as Quince and Co are around, we cannot get too lost in the world of the forest, since we are always being reminded that we are watching a play being made. The *parody* of play-making makes the *work* of play-making directly visible.

Shakespeare's own skill as a playwright, showing off this masterpiece of complex construction with its multiple intersecting plot lines, is brought into view by these craftsmen rehearsing their play. The onstage incompetence provides one measure of the competence both of

James Cagney as Bottom and Joe E. Brown as Flute in a 1935 American film

the work that contains them and of the actors who perform it for us. As Patricia Parker has pointed out, the emphasis on construction and "joinery" in the performers' professions also draws our attention to the great variety of things that are "joined" by the play: men and women in marriage, humans and animals in Bottom's ass-head, mortals and immortals in Titania's love for him, words to one another in speeches by characters and by Shakespeare himself. We are invited to consider *how* these things are joined – skilfully or ineptly, freely or coerced, "natural" or "monstrous", and hence how we create the artificial institutions and social structures that contain and bind us.

When a bad play is being rehearsed by good actors playing bad actors, we can't avoid thinking about how plays of all kinds *work*: why they appeal to us and why we grant them authority over our feelings and thoughts. When Snout worries "Will not the ladies be afeared of the lion?" we laugh at the strangeness of our own tendency to be drawn into the action: to cry at tragedy and feel with and for characters, to be moved by what we see. How, exactly, does a play engage our attention so strongly when we know all

WALL AND LION

The wall in Ovid's "Pyramus and Thisbe", says James Calderwood, "stands for the prohibition of desire and its cranny for desire itself". In Peter Quince's production of "Pyramus and Thisbe" during the *Dream*, the wall becomes Wall – it can come down and make an exit, though several critics think that Shakespeare, taking his cue perhaps from Bottom's line about meeting in the wood to "rehearse most obscenely", exploits all the ribald potentialities of Ovid's wall. The critic Jon Lawson Hinely sums them up:

The thwarted sexual development and frustration of the lovers blocked by this recalcitrant wall is bawdily suggested by a hodgepodge of vaginal, phallic, and anal allusions... The wall suggests both the female and male sexual organs. The phrases the time that it is not a "real" event? In posing this question Shakespeare is exploring, from a different angle, the role of the imagination in our lives. It is important in drama too, as is evident from the way Theseus and his court laugh at the mechanicals' performance in the last act.

> HIPPOLYTA:
>> *This is the silliest stuff that ever I heard.*
>
> THESEUS:
>> *The best in this kind are but shadows; and the*
>> *worst are no worse, if imagination*

"the crannied hole, or chink", "the cranny", "right and sinister" and Pyramus's request that the "sweet and lovely wall,/ Show me thy chink" all allude to the female genitalia aspects of the wall (5.1). Thisbe, for her part, is unintentionally scatological when declaiming, "My cherry lips have often kissed thy stones,/ Thy stones with lime and hair knit up in thee", and "I kiss the wall's hole, not your lips at all."

Wall's blocking of sexual access, through which naughty giggles still escape, contrasts with the sudden and terrible violence of Lion – of whom "the duchess and the ladies" may well be afraid. With only a roar for wooing, Lion simply springs and preys, even if his only prize is Thisbe's mantle, her protective covering – perhaps the hymens about to be breached this same night in the marriage beds. Pyramus inadvertently points the implication when he laments that "Lion vile hath here deflowered my dear!" Between Wall and Lion, the fortunes of a happy sexual expression are beset with difficulties ∎

amend them.

It must be your imagination then, and not
theirs. (V.i)

Hippolyta's reply here shrewdly draws attention again to the audience's contribution to the success of any play. And even Hippolyta later finds herself drawn into the action, in spite of her own incredulity: "Beshrew my heart but I pity the man," she says of Bottom's performance, though whether she pities his lack of acting skill or the fate of Pyramus is not made clear.

The choice of the play the mechanicals stage is important too: "Pyramus and Thisbe" is like a dark version of what happens in the wood, reminding us, despite the comic incompetence of the actors, that passion can lead to the animal violence of sex and to suicide. The lamentable performance the mechanicals stage, with its unhappy ending, shows us that love can be a route to tragedy, that the night's goings-on in the wood could have ended very badly indeed. So Bottom's hapless line on finding Thisbe's bloody mantle – "Since lion vile hath here deflowered my dear" – raises a guffaw, but also points with grim humour to the wounding of love implicit in the myth of the western flower "now purple with love's wound". But so lightly is the connection drawn that, although *we* apprehend

Opposite: Judi Dench as Queen Elizabeth/Titania
in a 2010 production at the Rose Theatre, Kingston

it, the noble spectators whom it most concerns, in their negligent condescension, do not notice how they are implied in what they see.

What should we make of Titania and Bottom?

By far the most famous sequence in the play is the encounter between Titania and Bottom. Ask most people what they recall of the play, and the Fairy Queen and the Weaver in one another's arms, each under a separate spell, is the likely response. In some ways, the image of their encounter has come to stand as an emblem of the whole thrust of Shakespeare's imagination, with its delight in the energies unleashed by strange, indecorous, even scandalous juxtapositions – kings with clowns, tragedy with comedy, laments with puns.

The image of Titania and Bottom is also the aspect of the play that has occasioned the most controversy, both on stage and among the critics, largely through the question of how sexual it is. Jan Kott, the influential Polish critic who in 1964 declared *"Shakespeare Our Contemporary"*, seized especially on this scene, and it became an icon of theatrical as well as sexual liberation, particularly in the hands of the director Peter Brook, who had Bottom paraded shoulder-high about the stage with one of the (very adult) fairies miming sexual excitement with an outstretched arm rising with fist clenched from between Bottom's legs, all to the tune of Mendelssohn's famous "Wedding March". Kott described the play in terms of "the dark sphere of sex, where there is no more beauty and ugliness; there is only infatuation and liberation"; he saw in the *Dream* not reason's redemption of depravity but an energetic celebration of the night world of desire, with all its powerful compulsions. Kott's account of the ass and the fairy queen likewise assumes that complete release from sexual repression and constraint is the main point of the play's idea of dreaming:

> The slender, tender and lyrical Titania longs for animal love. Puck and Oberon call the transformed Bottom a monster. The frail and sweet Titania drags the monster to bed, almost by force. This is the lover she wanted and dreamed of; only she never wanted to admit it, even to herself. Sleep frees her from inhibitions. The monstrous ass is being raped by the poetic Titania, while she keeps on chattering about flowers.

This vigorous image of fantasy sex certainly makes for lively theatrical fun, and contemporary productions often depict an eagerly sexual romp. But the text is not at all explicit about it. Quite the contrary. This is worth thinking about, since Shakespeare was perfectly capable of giving the scene more directly bawdy language had he chosen to. William Empson put the question carefully, and his summary is worth bearing in mind. Kott, he said,

> is ridiculously indifferent to the letter of the play and labours to befoul its spirit. And yet the [more innocent] Victorian attitude to it also feels oppressively false, and has a widespread influence... If the genital action is in view, nobody denies that the genitals of Bottom remained human. The first audience would not have admired Bottom, and nor would I, for letting the thing go so far if unwilling to respond. The sequence is sadly short.

In other words, there is a lot of possibility and no certainty – and the matter is not overly important. It may be that the point of the scene is less sexual liberty than lyrical and comic freedom.

Bottom is the only character who literally undergoes a metamorphic change, with his acquisition of an ass-head. "Bless thee, Bottom! Bless thee! thou art translated!" says Peter Quince, using another word for Ovid-like metamorphosis, though Bottom's change does not come from Ovid but from a later ancient writer, Apuleius. But here, where Shakespeare gets closest to a direct staging of an Ovid-like divine-human meeting, we get comic drama instead of erotic violence. The ridiculous ass-head is not an outgrowth

of Bottom's inordinate desire, but a practical
joke played on him by Puck to make fun of his
foolishness – a joke that Bottom himself doesn't get
since he hardly ever seems to notice he has such a
head.

The difference from Ovid's type of "translation"
points to a crucial change that Shakespeare
makes in what he does with Ovid's work. As
Jonathan Bate points out, where Ovid explores

APULEIUS

Apuleius was a Latin author
of the second century A.D.
who was born and spent
much of his life in Roman
North Africa, though he
also travelled to Athens for
study. Like his later African
compatriot, St Augustine,
he was a rhetorician
and philosopher. Unlike
Augustine, who attacked
his philosophical writings,
he was a committed
pagan. His most famous
work is, like Ovid's, titled
The Metamorphoses, but it
is now more often known
as *The Golden Ass*. It is the
only complete surviving
work of Latin prose fiction.
It tells of a young man,
Lucius, who experiments
with magic for erotic
purposes and is accidentally
turned into an ass. After
many adventures in the
lower orders of society
in the Roman Empire,
including being the object of
a rich woman's lurid sexual
attention, he is returned to
human form at a religious
festival of the goddess Isis
and becomes her devotee.
The book was available in
both Latin and English to
Shakespeare ∎

the vulnerability and plasticity of what we can be through myth, Shakespeare uses drama. Bottom with the ass's head is a wonderful occasion for the actor playing him (and for the actress playing Titania) to perform a comic scene in which they share with the audience a piece of make-believe, of superbly indulgent *acting*. Critics who take the transformation too seriously, like Kott, run the risk of missing its rich comedy and the audience's usual response to it: delighted laughter. What is celebrated is not so much the free energy of sexual liberation – even in productions that have the pair

THE LEGEND OF THE MINOTAUR

The centre of the play's imaginative world – the beguiling scene between Bottom and Titania – is like a happy version of one of the strongest classical images of erotic monstrosity: the story of Pasiphae, Queen of Crete,

and the Bull of Poseidon. As punishment for some transgression, the gods cause Queen Pasiphae, the wife of Minos, to desire sex with a magnificent bull belonging to her husband's herd. The Queen appeals for help to the great inventor-artist, Daedalus, who constructs a cow-disguise which she then uses to seduce the bull. The result of the union is the famous Minotaur, a man with the head of a bull.

Horrified by the monster, Minos imprisons it in another of Daedalus's inventions, the "labyrinth" –

copulating on stage or hotly exiting with intent – as the free energy of the theatre. Of course, the two often feed off one another, as Shakespeare knew very well, and staged for good and bad in such plays as *As You Like It* and *Antony and Cleopatra*.

Watch Bottom and Titania at play and you can immediately see that, though a strong erotic feeling is present, its temper is more relaxed and comically indulgent than fervent and sensual:

TITANIA:
Come, sit thee down upon this flowery bed,

a huge maze of tunnels from which no one can escape. To the hidden monster is fed regularly a "tribute" of young people sent from Athens. One day, some years later, Theseus comes with the tribute party and, with the help of Minos's daughter, Ariadne, kills the Monster in his labyrinth. Ariadne flees with him, but he later abandons her on the island of Naxos.

This tale is there in the play as if glimpsed out of the corner of an eye. "My mistress with a monster is in love," giggles Puck when Titania begs for the ass-headed Bottom's love. And the lovers in the wood feel they are trapped in some sort of labyrinth, one that may include their own desires. Theseus, of course, does not kill Bottom – though he ridicules him when he appears as an actor and dies on stage – but the echo suggests how Shakespeare is thinking throughout his play of the implications of Theseus's history as a hero of both reason and violence, both a rational ruler and a serial seducer ∎

The painter Richard Dadd at work on Contradiction:
Oberon and Titania, *c. 1856 (see below)*

TEN FACTS
ABOUT *A MIDSUMMER NIGHT'S DREAM*

1.

The play is the subject of a number of paintings, particularly Victorian fairy paintings. The artist most closely associated with ths genre is Richard Dadd. Travelling up the Nile in 1842, Dadd underwent a dramatic personality change; becoming delusional and violent, he believed himself to be under the influence of the Egyptian God Osiris. Recuperating in 1843, he murdered his father, convinced that he was the devil in disguise, then fled for France, attempting to kill another tourist en route. He produced his subsequent work in Bethlehem hospital and Broadmoor. Other artists to have produced works inspired by the play include William Blake, Henry Fuseli and Edwin Landseer.

2.

Titania's great speech on the foul weather and the dislocation of the seasons may reflect the actual weather while Shakespeare was writing the *Dream*. Contemporary accounts suggest 1594 was memorably bad from March onwards. According to one diary account: "June and July were very wet and wonderfull cold like winter, that the 10 dae of Julii many did sit by the fyer... There were many great fludes this summer..." The summers of 1595 and 1596 are also supposed to have been cold and wet.

3.

An anonymous adaptation of *A Midsummer Night's Dream* forms the libretto of Purcell's *The Fairy Queen* (1692). Following his death in 1695 the score was lost and rediscovered only in the early 1900s. Gustav Holst conducted the first modern performance in 1911. Purcell did not set the text to music, rather composing "Act Tunes", music for short masques after every act but the first. Recent scholarship suggests that the opera was composed for the 15th wedding anniversary of William and Mary.

4.

Benjamin Britten wrote an opera, first performed in 1960, and in 2000 Elvis Costello composed the music for a full-length ballet, *Il Sogno*, based on the play. The play is also the inspiration for Felix Mendelssohn's orchestral suite of the same name.

A Midsummer Night's Dream was George Balanchine's first original full-length ballet, premiered in 1962.

5.

In April 1964, The Beatles performed the Pyramus and Thisbe play-within-a-play from *A Midsummer Night's Dream* for a TV special in honour of Shakespeare's 400th birthday. Paul McCartney (Pyramus), John Lennon (Thisbe), George Harrison (Moonshine) and Ringo Starr (Lion) performed alongside friends who played Lysander, Hippolyta, Demetrius and Theseus (see p.105).

6.

When the mechanicals say they fear bringing in "a lion among ladies", Shakespeare may have been recalling an event he almost certainly knew about. At a royal feast in Scotland in 1594, a chariot was drawn in by a "blackamoor" while King James was at dinner. According to one account, the chariot "should have been drawn by a lyon, but because his presence might have brought some feare to the nearest" it was thought better to engage the black servant instead.

7.

British astronomer William Herschel named the two moons of Uranus he discovered in 1787 after characters in the play, Oberon and Titania. Another moon, named Puck, was discovered by *Voyager* in 1985. All of the 27 known moons of Uranus are named after characters from the works of Shakespeare and Alexander Pope.

8.

Some Shakespeare scholars think the *Dream* was written to grace a wedding in a noble household. Harold Brooks, editor of the Arden *Dream*, is among those who opt for the marriage of Elizabeth Carey and Thomas, son of Henry, Lord Berkeley, on 19 February 1596. This took place in Blackfriars. Elizabeth was a granddaughter of the lord chamberlain, the patron of Shakespeare's acting company. She was also one of Queen Elizabeth's goddaughters, but it is not known whether the Queen herself attended the wedding.

9.

The *Dream*, as the critic Shirley Nelson Garner has noted, is a rewarding subject for students of same-sex desire, or so-called "queer theory", thanks to Hippolyta's Amazonian identity, the relationship between Hermia and Helena and the bond between Titania and her votary.

10.

The name Oberon originated in the early 13th century. A fairy dwarf, Oberon, assists the eponymous hero of *Huon de Bordeaux*, a French *chanson de geste*. Shakespeare may have known the French heroic song through John Bourchier's translation (c.1540). Oberon the fairy also appears in Robert Greene's play *James IV* (c.1590). In Philip Henslowe's diary there is also note of a performance of a play, *Hewen of Burdocize*, on December 28, 1593.

> *While I thy amiable cheeks do coy,*
> *And stick musk-roses in thy sleek smooth*
> > *head,*
> *And kiss thy fair large ears, my gentle joy.*
> BOTTOM:
> *Where's Peaseblossom?*
> PEASEBLOSSOM:
> *Ready.*
> BOTTOM:
> *Scratch my head Peaseblossom. (IV.i)*

Bottom wants food, music and sleep, not sexual relations. "Of all the many incongruities in this episode," observes Edward Berry, "the subtlest, least expected, and most characteristically Shakespearian, is the bestial lover's lack of interest in sex." Titania, for her part, wants to kiss his ears, not other parts, however we might think ears *stand for* other parts. In some ways, the scene might be rather less strange if it were just naughty, even obscene. Instead, it is blithe and lyrical, unaware of the fierce call of Kott's "animal love" (even Kott has to concede that Bottom "is more interested in the frugal pleasure of eating than in the bodily charms of Titania"). Throughout, Bottom behaves with admirable comic dignity and even, paradoxically, a measure of what Theseus might call "cool reason". His imperviousness to both the blandishments of love and the oddity of his situation is marvellously comic. He expands into his sudden promotion as if to the manner born:

BOTTOM:
> *I cry your worship's mercy, heartily: I beseech*
> *your worship's name.*

COBWEB:
> *Cobweb.*

BOTTOM:
> *I shall desire you of more acquaintance, good*
> *Master Cobweb: if I cut my finger, I shall*
> *make bold with you. Your name, honest*
> *gentleman?*

PEASEBLOSSOM:
> *Peaseblossom.*

BOTTOM:
> *I pray you, commend me to Mistress Squash,*
> *your mother, and to Master Peascod, your*
> *father. Good Master Peaseblossom, I shall*
> *desire you of more acquaintance too. (III.i)*

Balanced between parody and dignity, the scene
rewards a high degree of skill in a comic actor.
Our gaze upon Bottom in his perfect ease is
as indulgent as the author's in giving it to him,
and the actor knows it. What looks grotesque
to outside observers (like Oberon and Puck) is
realised from within as warmth, generosity and
companionship. As Titania and Bottom drift
towards sleep, she lulls him:

So doth the woodbine the sweet honeysuckle
Gently entwist; the female ivy so
Enrings the barky fingers of the elm. (IV.i)

The image of woodbine with honeysuckle
shows a partnership of equals – the two plants
are essentially the same, twisted around each
other. The second image, of the female ivy that
"enrings" the elm, imagines a kind of natural
marriage, with the male even wearing the ring.
Both together suggest alternatives at odds with
the standard Elizabethan image of marriage,
realised in the freedom of the night's imagination,
where the world of rulers and their "cool reason" is
suspended. It is these images of possibility, rather
than Kott's of "animal love", that occupy the heart
of the play's fantasy.

Titania's response to Bottom also replays
aspects of her feeling for the stolen Indian boy,
whose place he takes in her affections. The boy, we
are told, she "crowns... with flowers, and makes...
all her joy", while Bottom's temples are "rounded/
With a coronet of fresh and fragrant flowers".
By including these recollections of her love for
the Indian boy, the scene again makes the point
that even in imagination we love in the way our
personality has prepared us to, if also in ways that
reveal parts of that personality with which we may
be less acquainted, or even less comfortable.
Love for Titania is always, in part, maternal love,

Calista Flockhart as Helena, Christian Bale as Demetrius, Dominic West as Lysander and Anna Friel as Hermia, in Michael Hoffman's 1999 film.

a warmth of feeling elsewhere absent from the play. Notably, she does not ever speak of her love for Oberon.

But though we may long for dream or desire to release the unexpected for us, the play doubts our ability to sustain very much unless it suits some daylight purpose. And that purpose in the play is Oberon's, as we are repeatedly reminded. Even while Titania and Bottom are delighting one another, from outside their magic circle her choice is always regarded with a mixture of disgust and amusement. Puck recounts the matter in gleeful tones to Oberon ("Titania waked and straightway loved an ass!"); Oberon enjoys having his malice satisfied ("This falls out better than I could devise"), and refers to Bottom as a "hateful fool". He recounts how he has taunted the enchanted Titania, presumably with her degraded taste, while she "in mild terms begg'd my patience". But having obtained the Indian boy and humiliated his Queen, he releases "this hateful imperfection of her eyes", commanding her to "be as thou wast wont to be". Awakened and restored to her dignity, Titania pushes her "dream" away in dismay. Apparently, the experience is to leave no lasting trace.

Still, Oberon's sense of the hatefulness and indignity of these scenes forms no part of what we are actually presented with on stage. And if Titania is appalled by her night's dalliance, Bottom has an altogether different feeling for it. It amazes and perplexes him, suggesting a world beyond his imagining:

> *I have had a most rare vision. I have had a dream, past the wit of man to say what dream it was: man is but an ass, if he go about to expound this dream. Methought I was – there is no man can tell what. Methought I was, – and methought I had, – but man is but a patched fool, if he will offer to say what methought I had. The eye of man hath not heard, the ear of man hath not seen, man's hand is not able to taste, his tongue to conceive, nor his heart to report, what my dream was. (IV.i)*

Amidst this jumble of the senses traces of his dream still cling to him, in ways he cannot quite perceive, though he feels they have great significance. He even echoes St Paul's famous description of "the bottom of God's secrets", which said: "Eye hath not seen, neither ear hath heard, neither came into the man's heart, [the things] which God hath prepared for them that love him" (*I Corinthians* 2: 9). Deep things seem to Bottom to have been in his dream. Even his garbling of the Bible has its own daft magnificence. In the world of dreams, eyes may hear, ears may see, the upside-down world may reveal truths unguessed at in daylight. "Bottom's Dream" – which has no bottom – is his rich image of the potential of dreaming as a source of unending imaginative possibility.

Bottom gropes for a proper way of expressing this vision, but he cannot hang on to it and, in the end, falls into dumbness. Only the possibility of its transmutation into some sort of artwork remains in his idea of the ballad of "Bottom's Dream", to be written by Peter Quince. Bottom imagines singing it "in the latter end of a play before the Duke" but we hear no more about it, unless perhaps it was to be the "Epilogue" to the play of Pyramus and Thisbe that Theseus, eager for his wedding bed, declines to hear. Instead, what we get is Bottom's sense of the wonderful character of his own experience in touching such unexpected mystery. Coming out of his blessed night, he expresses most vividly the sense that all the wakers have of what theatre critic Michael Billington calls a "transfigured strangeness", the central feeling of the play.

How are women treated in the play?

The world of *A Midsummer Night's Dream*, is a patriarchal one. Among the mortals, Theseus is in charge; he speaks first; he enforces Egeus's paternal demand that Hermia marry *his* choice of spouse. Among the fairies, Oberon demands submission from his Queen. The very form of Shakespeare's comedy, with its steady drive towards marriage, restricts what the women can and can't look forward to.

In this play, the expectation of marriage is the opening subject of the dialogue. Hermia's argument with her father, for all her insistence on her right to choose, is over *whom* she will marry, not over *whether* she will marry. Though Theseus briefly refers to an unmarried life as one of Hermia's options – "to live a barren sister all your life/ Chanting faint hymns to the cold fruitless moon" – the choice, however virtuous, is not presented as attractive. Hermia does not disagree. Wishing to disentangle herself from her father's blunt authority, with its insistence that "As she is mine I may dispose of her", she longs only to fling herself into the arms and household of her chosen male. As feminist critics have rightly argued, Shakespeare's comedies safeguard the world of the play for regular marriage. Some plays raise doubts about this outcome, but none disavows it altogether. In the last act, having achieved its marital goal, *A Midsummer Night's Dream* gives its female characters very little to say – and Hermia and Helena nothing at all.

Indeed all the women in the play are notably limited in their sexual and social roles; all are married or about to be married; there is a striking absence of women of authority. There are no mothers in the *Dream*, as James Calderwood points out, and the house of the "widow aunt" which offers sanctuary for lovers outside the jurisdiction of Athens is never reached. The independent society of the Amazons has been defeated, and the one powerful woman who does assert herself, Titania, is promptly made the object of "torment for this injury" by Oberon.

AMAZONS

In Greek mythology, the Amazons were a nation of all-female warriors. Amazon women are supposed to have cut off one of their breasts in the interests of more efficient archery and disdained marriage. (The name Amazon was explained by the Greeks as meaning "without a breast".) According to myth, once a year, to prevent their race from dying out, they visited a neighbouring tribe for purely reproductive purposes. Male children from these unions were either killed, sent back to their fathers or exposed in

At the same time, the women characters are presented much more fully and interestingly than the men. The asymmetry and frank subordination of their fate as women results paradoxically in Shakespeare paying them much more poetic attention: complex fates elicit complex responses, and it is clear that the women in the play's world sacrifice a great deal more than their men when they marry, with their husbands becoming, in effect, their spokesmen if not their controllers. Two examples of this comparative depth are especially striking, and both explore the richness of a world of female intimacy presented by the play as especially fragile, and valuable in part because of that very fragility. The sense of loss the women feel in both cases is very poignant, and

the wilderness to fend for themselves. The female children were brought up by their mothers.

Another version of the myth has it that when the Amazons went to war they did not kill all their male opponents, taking some as slaves with whom, once or twice a year, they would have sex. Classical myth used the Amazons as a society against which male heroes could measure themselves to establish their superiority. One of the twelve Labours of Hercules was to steal a rich belt belonging to Hippolyta, Queen of the Amazons. And one of the sculpted friezes on the Parthenon, the temple of Athena in ancient Athens, depicted the fight between Theseus and the Amazons – like the Persians an army of foreign invaders whom Athenian might had defeated ∎

Shakespeare explores it with more sensitivity and psychological depth than he does the plight of any of the male characters.

The first example is Titania's narrative of the Indian Boy in Act Two, Scene One. The Indian Boy, whom we never see directly, is an attendant of Titania's described by Puck as "a lovely boy stolen from an Indian King". Oberon wants him as "knight of his train, to trace the forests wild". Fairies were notorious stealers of human babies, but why should the play import this changeling from so great a distance?

The distance may be the point. For one thing, it expands what Titania calls the "fairy kingdom" to encompass the whole world, just as Puck offers to "put a girdle round about the earth in forty minutes" and Oberon claims that "we the globe

EXOTIC INDIA

For England under Elizabeth, "India" was mostly a place of legend, rumour and speculation. Few people knew where the lands now known as "India" actually were. "The Indies", both East and West, seemed impossibly remote and exotic. English traders had little direct contact with the Indian subcontinent, whose goods – especially textiles and spices, the latter often in turn traded from further

can compass soon/ Swifter than the wandering moon" and has come to the wood of Athens from "the farthest step of India". Such range and velocity increases the imaginative power the fairies bring to the play's dreamable world. The fairy exotic has a global reach.

But Titania's narrative of the boy may give a further reason for his Indian origin. Titania, it emerges, is refusing to give Oberon the boy not only because she wants to assert her right to control her staff. The boy has a specific, personal significance to her. "His mother," she tells us "was a votaress of my order", that is, one of Titania's particular devotees:

And, in the spicèd Indian air, by night,
Full often hath she gossiped by my side,

East – traditionally reached England only along a route that might include Persian, Arabic, Egyptian, Venetian, Dutch and French intermediaries.

Direct trade was an object of growing interest, however. That later giant of imperial trade and domination, the English East India Company, was given its charter in 1600, about five years after *A Midsummer Night's Dream* appeared, and the romance of the mercantile sea trade to India figures in the play: "the embarkèd traders on the flood" have a kind of imaginative resonance that comes through Titania's description. India is already a place of rich fantasy, as it would be for centuries afterwards ∎

And sat with me on Neptune's yellow sands,
Marking the embarkèd traders on the flood,
When we have laughed to see the sails conceive
And grow big-bellied with the wanton wind;
Which she, with pretty and with swimming gait
Following, her womb then rich with my young
squire,

Would imitate, and sail upon the land
To fetch me trifles, and return again,
As from a voyage, rich with merchandise.
But she, being mortal, of that boy did die;
And for her sake do I rear up her boy,
And for her sake I will not part with him. (II.i)

The scene of Titania and her Indian votaress is described with great lyrical power: they laugh and play on the sea-shore, mock the serious men's business of the sailing merchants, re-imagine the sea trade as a second-rate imitation of the joyful freight of pregnancy. But the votaress dies; the happy time is destroyed by death; Titania's tone turns sad. Only the boy remains to her. As long as she has him, he will remind her of her lost friend: "for her sake," she says, she "will not part with him". He is, in effect, a kind of dream substitute for her loss, the last trace of a deep experience of female companionship and mutual devotion. Making him an *Indian* boy may, in addition to stressing the global world of fairy, be a way of putting this joyous idyll of female intimacy outside

*A 1964 National Youth Theatre production. The four lovers are
Helen Mirren as Helena, David Taylor as Demetrius, Diana Quick as
Hermia, and Andrew Murray as Lysander.*

the known and ordinary world, making it distant
and exotic, like the community of barbarian
female Amazons Theseus has recently defeated.

The other major instance of lost female
companionship in the play comes in Act Three,
Scene Two, when Helena laments the loss of
intimate companionship with Hermia and the
way it has had to yield to new heterosexual
commitments. As early as the first scene, Helena
tells Hermia she longs "to be to you translated",

81

as though becoming Hermia could substitute for losing her to Lysander. Anger against Hermia also seems partly the motive of Helena's betrayal of her friend's secrets (betrayal for betrayal, perhaps) – especially since telling Demetrius is precisely the opposite of an action in her own interest. Her sense of her contradictory position is expressed in unhappy paradoxes: betrayal is "a dear expense" that will only "enrich my pain".

Coleridge found this "ungrateful treachery" offensive, and grumped that it was "too true a picture of the lax hold that principles have on the

THE *DREAM* AND *ROMEO AND JULIET*

The relationship between *A Midsummer Night's Dream* and another of Shakespeare's early plays, *Romeo and Juliet*, has always interested critics.

We do not know exactly when the two plays were written, or which came first, but evidence points to 1595 or 1596 for both. In some ways they are like a pair. In both, love is the central topic. Both involve a prince trying to manage a social dispute that is disrupting the community. Each play seems to include a small version of the other inside it.

Thus in *Romeo and Juliet*, Mercutio, Romeo's friend, speaks of "Queen Mab", a tiny fairy "no bigger than an agate-stone" who causes people to have strange dreams. Sleeping female heart". But this seems entirely to overlook the sympathetic way Helena is portrayed. Indeed, if she seems truly to love anyone in the play, it would seem to be Hermia, with whom her deepest sense of herself is entwined; in the muddle of the wood, her real sense of grievance emerges when she laments what Hermia's "betrayal" has done to their old love:

> *We, Hermia, like two artificial gods,*
> *Have with our needles created both one flower,*
> *Both on one sampler, sitting on one cushion,*

lovers "dream of love", and ladies "straight on kisses dream". According to Mercutio, dreams are "the children of an idle brain,/ Begot of nothing but vain fantasy", which sounds rather like Theseus. The word "dream" occurs frequently in *Romeo and Juliet*, as A.D. Nuttall points out. Mercutio uses it seven times in his Queen Mab speech, and the speech itself is a response to Romeo's claim that dreams are true).

In *A Midsummer Night's Dream*, conversely, the playlet of "Pyramus and Thisbe" resembles the central story of *Romeo and Juliet*. In both cases, parents' opposition to the young lovers leads to separation, and ends with their tragic deaths by misunderstanding. This reflects the darker side of *Dream* itself, where this fate could easily have overtaken the lovers in the wood. But the parallel with the Italian play is hard to overlook. In some ways, the two plays are inside-out versions of one another, exploring similar questions of sexual desire and its social effects from the opposed perspectives of comedy and tragedy ∎

Both warbling of one song, both in one key,
As if our hands, our sides, voices and minds,
Had been incorporate. So we grew together,
Like to a double cherry, seeming parted,
But yet an union in partition;
Two lovely berries moulded on one stem;
So, with two seeming bodies, but one heart;
Two of the first, like coats in heraldry,
Due but to one and crowned with one crest.
And will you rent our ancient love asunder,
To join with men in scorning your poor friend?
It is not friendly, 'tis not maidenly:
Our sex, as well as I, may chide you for it,
Though I alone do feel the injury. (III.ii)

This is a sweet picture. And yet a moment later Helena is begging the men to defend her from a totally different knowledge of Hermia, who "was a vixen when she went to school" and who, "though she be but little, she is fierce". Under the pressure of competing love, the past of the girls splits in two – into a utopia of childhood pleasures and a hell of playground spatting.

Which is the true image of what they have been? The two versions have both been there all along, presumably, but the play has forced them for the first time into clear opposition. Helena both laments the lost unity and uses the discovered knowledge of their difference to her advantage. And the tension between these versions of her

Still from Lindsay Kemp's 1984 film featuring Michael Matou. The production emphasised the masque-like qualities of the play.

history, in addition to being comic, allows her – alone of the four – to glimpse a complexity to selfhood, its division against itself in the loss of a happy and stable singleness. Helena calls this self-knowledge, sadly, her "folly":

> *And now, so you will let me quiet go,*
> *To Athens will I bear my folly back*
> *And follow you no further; let me go:*

You see how simple and how fond I am. (III.ii)

These evocations of lost female intimacy are perhaps the richest speeches of the play – there are no such scenes among the men – and their emotional tone contrasts sharply with the central goings-on, in which the men largely get their way. They underline the centrality of loss to women's experience in a way that reinforces the asymmetry of "giving up" entailed by marriage itself. So if the play, like all Shakespeare's comedies, invests in marriage as a goal and a benefit, it also suggests by this asymmetry in the handling of women characters that their experience of love and

OTHER SHAKESPEAREAN DREAMERS

In Shakespeare, dreams can be a guide to character. Guilty consciences often show themselves in dreams, as with Richard III or Macbeth and Lady Macbeth, who all have bad dreams that, in Macbeth's words, "shake us nightly".

But stranger things can happen in dreams too. The Duke of Clarence, whom Richard is plotting to murder, has a dream in which he imagines his brother Richard "accidentally" pushing him off a boat to drown. His dreaming mind tries to tell him something it knows, which his waking mind cannot bring itself to see – that his brother will kill him. The dreams of marriage is quite different from that of the men who are their lovers and husbands.

Why is the play called a dream?

The title, *A Midsummer Night's Dream,* is something of a puzzle. Are we to imagine it is we who are having the dream, or Shakespeare, or some of the characters? Shakespeare's audiences saw his works in the afternoon, in natural light, not in a darkened theatre with artificial spotlights directing their attention. A waking dream in broad

Caliban, Propero's slave in *The Tempest,* are full of music and make him cry with longing for a world of freedom and beauty that his waking life, and his master, keep from him. More intriguing still is the newly-crowned King Henry V, who calls his past life as the rude-boy Prince Hal a dream, and banishes Falstaff, his disreputable knight companion:

I long have dreamed of such
a kind of man,
So surfeit-swelled, so old and
so profane;
But being awaked, I do
despise my dream.

Despising a dream, rather than fearing or loving or pondering it, is a complex attitude to take. It means not just refusing and casting out what may be some inkling of your personality, but taking up a militant disgust towards it. Henry the King may feel, and even be, the better for despising his dream life, but Hal the person has to censure himself severely to make the transition ∎

daylight is a stranger beast than something we experience in a dark room.

So Shakespeare's title raises the question of what a dream is worth, and to whom. Dreams are fragile; they are deeply private, and remembering them – let alone sharing them with others – can quickly lead to frustration. But they are powerful stories we tell ourselves when we are at our least guarded – or that something tells us, something which we may feel is *not* really quite ourselves.

Sigmund Freud, the greatest investigator of dreams in modern times, called dreams "the royal road to the unconscious" and invented a powerful inner agent to account for our frequent sense that we do not dream so much as we *are dreamed*. He named that agent or power "the It" ("das Es" in German), now usually known in English as "the Id". Freud's "It" is direct and visceral – it is that place or entity inside me which I do not want to acknowledge, both me and not-me, "mine own and not mine own". The "It" is where our deepest, least recognisable and acceptable desires live their fierce buried life, and our dreams are a cave of magic shadows into which we venture by night to make contact with selves we may not otherwise acknowledge.

Shakespeare had never heard of Freud's "It", of course, but he was well aware (as Freud himself conceded) that we can live quite different lives in sunlight and shadow. In Shakespeare's play, the strange transmuting process of dreaming becomes the name for a waking experience we have together in the theatre.

The only actual dream presented in the play is Hermia's at the end of Act Two. She and Lysander, having lost their way, decide to sleep in the wood and finish their journey in the morning. Lysander wants to sleep close alongside Hermia: "one turf shall serve as pillow for us both,/ One heart, one bed, two bosoms and one troth". She wishes them to sleep apart, and asks him to "lie further off, in human modesty". She seems concerned about what might happen in the night to two lovers lying close beside one another. Lysander presses his claim, insisting his love gives him the right to closer "bed-room" but at the same time insists his intentions are honest: "For lying so, Hermia, I do not lie."

But Lysander's pun interprets Hermia's fear for us: passionate young men may make promises they won't keep. Hermia resists and gets her way, praying that "Thy love ne'er alter til thy sweet life end". Gracious, if disappointed, Lysander replies: "Amen to that fair prayer". So they rest apart on the forest floor. And while they sleep, Puck mistakenly puts Lysander under the magic flower-spell and he wakes to fall in love with Helena and leave Hermia asleep on the ground. As he departs, Hermia awakes from a simple but devastating nightmare and calls out to him: "Help me, Lysander, help me!... Methought a serpent ate my heart away,/ And you sat smiling at his cruel prey." But, to her horror, Lysander is gone.

Hermia's dream clearly matches her situation: a woman with fears about her lover's trustworthiness sees those fears realised in a dream where she is viciously and intimately attacked and he only smiles: his love *has* altered. Her dream vividly responds to both her doubts about Lysander and her anxiety about impending sex with him. In the dream both she and Lysander are themselves and not themselves – she a helpless victim, he a smiling sadist, whose bestial agent attacks the centre of her being. Her dream releases and makes recognisable in a new way a whole knot of her compacted thoughts and feelings. It is not necessarily "true" – though it later seems to a horrified Hermia to come true. But it is *one* truth about her interior world. So dreams may be trying, in their peculiar way, to tell us something we know, but perhaps do not *wish* to know or cannot directly know.

If there is only the one *actual* dream in the play, the night-world of the wood makes the characters who experience it *think* they have been dreaming, because their experience is so strange and inscrutable. Bottom thinks this of his night's adventure. So too do the four lovers, who find their daylight lives scrambled by emotions of love and hatred for the "wrong" people. Waking, they use a language for what they have been through which beautifully captures the perplexing, evanescent quality of a dream:

DEMETRIUS:
> *These things seem small and*
> > *undistinguishable,*
> *Like far-off mountains turned into clouds.*

HERMIA:
> *Methinks I see these things with parted eye*
> *Where everything seems double.*

HELENA:
> > *So methinks;*
> *And I have found Demetrius like a jewel:*
> *Mine own and not mine own. (IV.i)*

Since they have fought and insulted and betrayed one another, one can imagine there is some nervousness about recalling details; they recede to the horizon of awareness. "These things" is as close as they come to naming them. At the same time, Helena's wonder at her discovery of Demetrius's revived love for her expresses the simultaneous possession and dispossession of ourselves we experience in dreaming, in the theatre, and in love.

Shakespeare's play, then, is called a dream because it explores how strange and unpredictable our own lives can sometimes seem. It is also more self-consciously interested in how art can reveal the secret workings of the daylight world, as dreams reveal these same secrets in a different way. In the forest, the characters become not so much who they are not, as who they might be, rehearsing versions of themselves that are hidden or implied in their ordinary lives: Demetrius relives his abandoned love for Helena (and ends up reviving it), Helena allows her envy and distrust of Hermia free reign ("She was a vixen when she went to school"), Lysander rebels against Hermia's restraint of his longings ("Get you gone, you minimus!"), Titania coddles a grown-up image of her Indian boy, and Bottom is a prince of the world's deep mysteries.

The play's richest image for what dreaming (and art, and theatre) offers us is kept half-hidden, like the work of dreaming itself, in Oberon's evocation of the Fairy Queen's "bower":

> *I know a bank where the wild thyme blows;*
> *Where oxlips and the nodding violet grows,*
> *Quite over-canopied with luscious woodbine,*
> *With sweet musk-roses and with eglantine.*
> *There sleeps Titania some time of the night,*
> *Lulled in sweet flowers, with dances and delight,*
> *And there the snake throws her enameled skin,*
> *Weed wide enough to wrap a fairy in. (II.i)*

This place of dreams is full of the energy of change: fertility suffuses it, the snake moults to grow there, the fairy wrapped in its skin may emerge as anything. Danger becomes art. The "wild thyme" of this place has a double meaning – "thyme" is even spelt "time" in the earliest versions of the play: it suggests this is a place of "wild time" that "blows" both like a flower opening and like the wind breathing. This bank where time blows wild and freely is as rich an evocation of dreaming as Shakespeare ever managed. That he places it here, at the site of the strangest encounter of his play – between the weaver and the Fairy Queen – says something about how richly he valued that strangeness. Shakespeare's drama is itself the "wild time" of which it speaks here, and the snake's enameled skin, like Prospero's magic garment in *The Tempest*, is a costume we can try on in our imaginations, to see what we may become if it fits.

Marjorie Garber says in her book on *Dream in Shakespeare*, that *A Midsummer Night's Dream* "reverses the categories of reality and illusion, sleeping and waking, art and nature, to touch upon the central theme of the dream which is truer than reality". But I think Shakespeare would see neither dreaming nor reality as "truer" than the other. A dream may reveal what is invisible to waking, but this does not mean waking is wrong or false; we live in the waking world as well. In dreams we think again, think differently; we are "ourselves and not ourselves". Throughout the action of his play, Shakespeare plays with strange transmutations of experience that look like, or feel like, dreaming, and that offer to illuminate waking reality from an unexpected, sometimes startling, angle.

How does the play's language reflect its view of love?

In 1679, John Dyden, who greatly admired Shakespeare, nevertheless complained that "many of his words, and more of his phrases, are scarce intelligible. And of those which we understand, some are ungrammatical, others coarse; and his whole style is so pestered with figurative expressions, that it is as affected as it is obscure." Dryden put these "errors" down to the unrefined state of the theatre and poetry in general in Shakespeare's day, allowing nevertheless that "it is almost a miracle that much of his language remains so pure; and that he who began dramatic poetry amongst us... should by the force of his own genius perform so much".

A century later, Dr Johnson voiced similar worries about the irregularity of Shakespeare's language, complaining especially of his tendency to pursue puns in what Johnson felt were excessive and indecorous ways. Puns were Shakespeare's "fatal Cleopatra, for which he lost the world and was content to lose it".

Yet while Shakespeare's puns were Johnson's bugbear, they do important work in his plays. When Lady Macbeth offers to smear blood on the faces of King Duncan's sleeping guards, she says: "I'll gild the faces of the grooms withal,/ For it must seem their guilt" (sounding like "they're gilt"). The pun on gild/guilt tells us a lot about Lady Macbeth: guilt is, she claims, something on the surface, like gilding, to put on and take off at will. She is, of course, very wrong, as her own terrible fate in the play will show, but framing the truth about the experience of guilt in an apparently casual pun – a grim little joke – is typical of Shakespeare's style.

Similarly, Lysander's nervous pun to Hermia in the wood – "lying so, fair Hermia, I do not lie" – points to what must be a crucial doubt for Hermia about her lover's sexual urgencies and his willingness to deceive in order to satisfy them. Her vulnerability as a young woman in love is summed up neatly and forcefully in his punning words.

In *A Midsummer Night's Dream*, Shakespeare is especially interested in what Stephen Fender calls the "double character" of words, with nothing being "quite as simple as it seems at first". But perhaps one should say "multiple" rather than "double". Words have complexities, overtones or undertones; sometimes we only half know what we mean, as though our words are in reality speaking us rather than we them, as though the speeches we make are formed by an agency not in our control, half-dreamed, "our own and not our own". Shakespeare's picture of language as unstable confirms and corresponds to his depiction of love as unstable. For Shakespeare, our very lives and our processes of thought and feeling – most of all, our loves – are, as Dryden complained of his poetry, "pestered" with figurative meanings. Helena, much of the time, is part-Hermia (as her name suggests) and part-Demetrius (as her feeling insists); Theseus's love woos "with my sword"; Bottom is Titania's Indian Boy, and also an ass.

Shakespeare's words are not fixed: they don't point clearly at single objects or concepts. A word for Shakespeare is often a knot of meaning where complex energies force their way into the world and on to our attention. *A Midsummer Night's Dream* makes this shimmering, ambiguous character of words the centre of its poetic effect. And, appropriately, the central image of the play is the equally elusive moon. Bathing everything in its ambiguous radiance, moonlight is itself, like language, figurative, since it only shines by reflecting, hence figuring, the absent sun. The moon is, we might say, the play's own figure of figuration.

This helps to explain why the moon attracts especially self-revelatory comment throughout the play – several characters uncover in the moon unexpected versions of themselves, versions

Fairies dance in the forest next to Puck, Oberon and Titania, Act IV Scene I,
William Blake, c.1785

that one suspects they do not quite understand.
Lysander, for example, hints that love is always
in part about oneself through his image of the
moon beholding, Narcissus-like, "her image in the
watery glass". And the play opens with Theseus
and Hippolyta both referring to the moon as they
discuss the delay to their wedding. Theseus sees
it as blocking him from his desires, like a rich old
woman ("a step-dame or a dowager") spending
a young man's inheritance by living too long. But
Hippolyta's moon is more subtle: "like to a silver
bow new-bent in heaven", it will "behold the night
of our solemnities". This suggests Hippolyta's
own about-to-be-lost life as a virgin warrior
and huntress, devoted to the moon-goddess,

Diana, whose bow her imagined new moon will recall. Hippolyta's moon has a mythic depth which Theseus's does not, just as her situation is more complex: a defeated warrior marrying her captor. The play's concerns with power, love, and surrender – both political and sexual – cluster around her in this opening moment. Hippolyta does not say what she thinks of her situation, but her moon says several things for her: loss, regret, expectancy, even displaced anger. The moon's bow is "new-bent" to shoot, but we do not hear at whom.

Theseus and Hippolyta, in telling us about the

NARCISSISM AND LOVE

Authors, critics and psychologists have long pondered the degree to which love for another is involved with love for oneself. Denis de Rougemont, in his *Passion and Society*, a history of love in western literature, speaks of love as "twin narcissism" and of lovers being "in love with their love". The psychoanalyst Helen Gediman puts it more prosaically, and obscurely. Love, she says, is "a more or less transient fusion state in which libidinal investment of the self is transferred to the object".

The Renaissance had its own perspective on this side of love. In his *Eros and Magic in the Renaissance*, Ioan Couliano says the lover "carves into his soul the model of the beloved.

moon, also tell us about themselves. All through the play, hidden feelings work their way into what a speaker makes of the moon, and whenever the moon appears, we should pay attention. So when Titania, later on, is preparing to carry Bottom away to her bower, she suddenly notices the moon, and comments:

> *The moon methinks looks with a watery eye;*
> *And when she weeps, weeps every little flower,*
> *Lamenting some enforcèd chastity.*
> *Tie up my love's tongue; bring him silently. (III.i)*

In that way, the soul of the lover becomes the mirror in which the image of the loved one is reflected." This is an image borrowed by the Renaissance directly from Plato, the great ancient theorist of love, for whom the lover "cannot account [for his affliction], not realising that his love is as it were a mirror in which he beholds himself". There are no mirrors in the *Dream*, but there is the moon, who "beholds her silvery image in the watery glass", and there is the lovers' awareness of themselves as each other's images:

Lysander speaks of his close similarity to Demetrius, Helena repeatedly emphasises her closeness, in fact or longing, to Hermia.

Renaissance love poetry made much of the lover's literal reflection in the eye of the beloved, as the two stare passionately into each other's eyes: even the most intimate view of the beloved was thus also a vision of the self. But the narcissistic element that composes love also makes us very vulnerable, as James Calderwood suggests: "When your I resides in another's eye,

She doesn't seem to realise how her own chastity is being "enforced" (that is, violated) at just this moment by the involuntary nature of her love, imposed by Oberon's spell. And yet her uneasy sense of the moon's sorrow *does* acknowledge her situation, in ways of which she remains unaware. As with Hermia's dream, there is more knowledge in the images of the moon than the speakers know how to extract.

Love and language in *A Midsummer Night's Dream* have certain traits in common. Both are powerful vehicles for self-expression and self-

an eye through which you see yourself as well, then you are partly split and alienated from yourself." This vulnerability, this risk, means loves can quickly turn to rage and hatred if it is rejected, as we see happen in the tangled relations of the four lovers. Jilting leads to loss of self respect and loss of love for the self. Calderwood writes:

> The annihilating looks and general antagonisms of the wood may remind us that falling in love is hard to distinguish from falling in hate. Coleridge noted that "Sympathy constitutes

friendship, but in love there is a sort of antipathy or opposing passion. Each strives to be the other" (*Table Talk*). Similarly, [Jacques] Lacan claims that lovers [may] find themselves flailing back and forth between love and hate, master and slave, victim and victimizer... [These views] seem perfectly illustrated by the lovers in the wood.

Modern psychoanalysis and criticism are thus replaying a complex of insights that are also visible in the subtleties of older texts like plays and poems, as far back as Greek philosophy ∎

realisation. But both can also escape the intentions and control of those through whom they flow, reshaping consciousness into unwonted, and sometimes unwanted, shapes. Both are profoundly metaphoric and metamorphic experiences, and both condense complicated histories into what may appear simple and local actions. A character's love, like a character's speech, always threatens to contain more than meets the eye. And the eye itself is not always reliable: as Hermia says after her night in the wood: "Methinks I see these things with parted eye,/ When everything seems double." Once again, as so often in Shakespeare, we find that the things we choose to express and realise ourselves, even our deepest needs and desires, disclose us in ways we do not have full control of. Language is a power that lives through us, even as we also find and speak ourselves through it.

How reassuring is the conclusion?

Lovers and rulers and players all emerge from their night in the wood with their sense of the world's goodwill transformed, indeed miraculously enhanced. Most of the characters can now achieve what they want to achieve: Theseus and Hippolyta to wed and rule, the young lovers to take their chosen partners, Bottom and his friends to keep their appointment with theatrical destiny. Oberon and Titania are "new in amity" and will shortly appear to bless and "dance in Duke Theseus's house triumphantly" for the end of the play. Everything has turned out well – except perhaps for Egeus, who has seen the Duke "overbear" his insistence that Hermia wed Demetrius. The former Athenian law, "which by no means we may extenuate", has proved in the end reasonably flexible. The dangerous parts of the night's experience are safely contained in the "tragical mirth" of Pyramus and Thisbe. The formerly brittle and abstract language of the lovers, as Stephen Fender argues, has developed a salutary flexibility and tentativeness. In the hands of Shakespeare and Oberon, twin pursuers of comic design, Jack now has his Jill once more. It is all very reassuring.

At the beginning of Act Five, in his usual rationalist way, Theseus puts the case that the story so far has been really a kind of nothing, a tissue of trivialities, only disturbing if one were foolish enough to take them seriously. In a speech to Hippolyta often taken as a statement of Shakespeare's own view of poetry, Theseus comments on the power of a lover's imagination:

HIPPOLYTA:

'Tis strange my Theseus, that these lovers speak of.

THESEUS:

> More strange than true: I never may believe
> These antique fables, nor these fairy toys.
> Lovers and madmen have such seething
> > brains,
> Such shaping fantasies, that apprehend
> More than cool reason ever comprehends.
> The lunatic, the lover and the poet
> Are of imagination all compact:
> One sees more devils than vast hell can hold,
> That is, the madman: the lover, all as frantic,
> Sees Helen's beauty in a brow of Egypt:
> The poet's eye, in a fine frenzy rolling,
> Doth glance from heaven to earth, from
> > earth to heaven;
> And as imagination bodies forth
> The forms of things unknown, the poet's pen
> Turns them to shapes and gives to airy
> > nothing
> A local habitation and a name.
> Such tricks hath strong imagination,
> That if it would but apprehend some joy,
> It comprehends some bringer of that joy;
> Or in the night, imagining some fear,
> How easy is a bush supposed a bear! (V.i)

The speech is famous as a piece of poetic rhetoric.
It is often taken as a defence or celebration of
the imagination, but it is rather an indictment
of it. Theseus insists that there is in the end no

substance to what the imagination produces – its shapes are "airy nothing". Poets, in Theseus's view, suffer from what the philosopher Alfred Whitehead called "misplaced concreteness": they make emotive statements about things that do not exist. Imagination is all "apprehension" – a sudden swift leaping of emotion into vivid statement – rather than the "comprehension" of "cool reason". It mistakes bushes for bears, not a wise thing to do. This is the Theseus of lordly poise and rational scepticism speaking.

That his speech has been taken as Shakespeare's own description of poetry is not without irony in a play whose commitment to imagination is announced in the title. Presumably Theseus would include dreamers in his list of nothing-knowers. As Graham Bradshaw points out, there is also more than a little irony in a figure who is himself an "antique fable" condemning fables for not being believable.

But typically, Theseus's opinion is immediately challenged, if, just as typically, the balance of the argument is uneven. Hippolyta is not so sure that what the lovers have gone through is delusion:

> *But all the story of the night told over,*
> *And all their minds transfigured so together,*
> *More witnesseth than fancy's images*
> *And grows to something of great constancy;*
> *But, howsoever, strange and admirable. (V.i)*

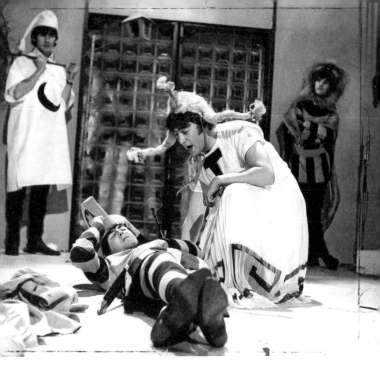

The Beatles act out a spoof of Act V Scene I to mark Shakespeare's Quatercentenery on their television programme Around The Beatles. *Paul McCartney plays Pyramus and John Lennon his lover Thisbe. Cilla Black featured as another act on the show. McCartney later owned a cat he named Thisbe.*

Conceding that "fancy's images" might be worth little, she nevertheless insists on the power of a shared story (including a play) to "transfigure" the mind and to produce unexpected and lasting effects. She speaks of the night's story as something that "grows" and compels attentive admiration, rather than dismissing it as a vacuous nothing. There is really no doubt which side of this dispute a poet is on, even one in a sceptical mood.

But though Titania's view of the events of the night as "strange and admirable" is more perceptive than Theseus's, doubts remain. Titania's question to Oberon – "Tell me how it came this night/ That I sleeping here was found/ With these mortals on the ground?" – remains unanswered. Or at least, his reply is kept judiciously offstage. Helena and Hermia say nothing at all after their marriages, though one might as easily conclude they are silent from overwhelming happiness. Egeus may or may not appear in the last act, depending on which surviving version of the play one chooses. (There are two, and this is one of

RHYME IN THE DREAM

In an interesting analysis in his lively *Doing Shakespeare*, Simon Palfrey says that rhyme in *A Midsummer Night's Dream* "is the medium of fantasy, dream, magic, rapture and transformation". The potentially catastrophic opening of the play, for example, is rendered "less threatening" by the lovers' reversion to rhyme, as in Lysander's

Helen, to you our minds we
will unfold:
Tomorrow night, when
Phoebe doth behold
Her silver visage in the wat'ry
glass,
Decking with liquid pearl the
bladed grass...

The rhyming couplets here "help create the play's distinctively permissive cocoon, one of nostalgia,

the few significant differences between them.)
If he does, he may or may not be resentful at
having his will over-ruled by the Duke. As in all
Shakespeare's comedies, the happiness of the
ending is a shadowed happiness.

Most troubling of all, perhaps, is the outcome
for Demetrius. Of course, he ends the play happy
in the arms of his Helena, his choice before his
first love for her "some heat from Hermia felt".
But it is important to remember that his renewed
commitment to Helena is *only* possible because
he remains undischarged from the magic flower's
spell, with what Oberon elsewhere calls its

escapism, and pastoral
experimentation. Indeed,
the forest itself works
rather like the rhymes
do: suggesting a buoyant
serendipity while in fact
pre-contracted to comi-
magic lore and its conflict-
dissolving symmetries".

More precisely, Palfrey
goes on, this "dream
forest" is the site of a battle
between disjunctive blank
verse – spoken, for instance,
by Titania and Helena in
their powerful speeches of
rebuke (II.i 81-119, III.ii
193-244), and in the vicious
catfight between Hermia

and Helena – and a "more
magical, passage-smoothing
rhyme", the chosen form of
Puck and Oberon and of the
lovers (including Bottom
and Titania) in their "often
confused raptures".

It is "telling", Palfrey
concludes, "that once the
spell is broken and the
lovers awake, they never
again speak in rhyme". But
though the lovers leave
rhyme behind, it "remains
the heartbeat of the play's
appeal, transferred at the
end into the oddly invincible
rhymes of Bottom's play and
Puck's magic" ▪

"hateful imperfection of [the] eyes". Critics like to provide comforting accounts of this wrinkle in the plot, pursuing the play's own interest in clarity and neatness. Frank Kermode puts it thus:

> Awake, [the lovers] see well enough: Demetrius abjures the dotage that enslaved him to Hermia and his love for Helena returns as 'natural taste' returns to a person cured of a sickness.

This is, of course, Demetrius's own account of what has happened. Yet are we entitled to credit him any more than we do Lysander when he tells Helena that "The will of man is by his reason swayed,/ And reason says you are the worthier maid"? In what sense is Demetrius's return to Helena "natural" rather than blatantly artificial – the arranged outcome of Oberon's normalising intervention? If Demetrius seemed "enslaved" to Hermia under the love-spell, so did Helena to him without it – rather more so, indeed. It is certainly *convenient* to accept Demetrius's account of his coming to "natural taste", as it neatly resolves the conflicts of the play. But one must simply abandon any attempt rigorously to distinguish "natural taste" from "dotage" in this case – what Demetrius now wants is still the product of the magical "love-in-idleness" flower; dotage and reason are simply two sides of the same coinage in the fluid currency of love.

A Midsummer Night's Dream is a comedy, and ends with a collective joy for the mortal lovers, and perhaps a sigh of relief. But comedy for Shakespeare is a bright and happy circle around which stand darker presences. In this play, Shakespeare makes the charmed circle of his comic vision abundantly clear by having his fairies beat its bounds at the end of the play. These mortals are, we are explicitly told, specifically "blest" and spared from all the sorts of harm that can befall mortal marriages. The palace of Theseus is to be filled with "glimmering light" and all the bridal beds visited in a ceremony of fairy magic so that "the issue there create/ Ever shall be fortunate". (Here those who remember the fate of Theseus's son Hippolytus may wonder how long fairy blessings last.) Likewise any bumps on the married road are to be smoothed in advance, for "So shall all the couples three,/ Ever true in loving be" and Theseus, the owner of the palace "Ever shall in safety rest".

These are happy words, but we are also reminded of what can all too easily happen without this pre-emptive blessing to turn away the quirks and waywardnesses of nature or fortune – all the "blots of Nature's hand" don't cease to exist simply because here they are banished. Meanwhile, outside the charmed circle, the fiercer predations of the natural and the supernatural world go on as always, even if humans are now oblivious to them. Puck evokes them directly as the dark time when "the hungry lion roars/ And the wolf behowls the moon" and when "the screech-owl, screeching loud/ Puts the wretch that lies in woe/ In remembrance of a shroud". Life may be starting in the bridal beds, the fairies that "follow darkness like a dream" may now be "frolic", but death stands outside the chamber door, and graves gape out their dead to haunt "the churchway paths". The lyric is beautiful, but it is made of darkness and death under a slippery moon. If this is our reassurance, we might feel we need more.

These ambivalences are laid out very cannily in Puck's Epilogue. Alone on stage, he is, in the end, the audience's servant, a messenger of the theatre company who are all dependent on our patronage for their survival. Like many epilogues of contemporary plays, it bows to our authority at once. We may not like the play. We may recoil from it and blight its prospects. Perhaps, for all the orderliness of its ending, it has travelled through waters too disturbing for some of us:

If we shadows have offended,
Think but this, and all is mended:
That you have but slumber'd here
While these visions did appear;
And this weak and idle theme,

No more yielding but a dream,
Gentles, do not reprehend:
If you pardon, we will mend.
And, as I am an honest Puck,
If we have unearned luck
Now to 'scape the serpent's tongue,
We will make amends ere long,
Else the Puck a liar call.
So, good night unto you all.
Give me your hands, if we be friends,
And Robin shall restore amends. (V.i)

This is strikingly apologetic even for an epilogue:
"mend" or "amend" appears four times in 16 lines,
suggesting the depth of Shakespeare's anxiety.
Puck's language in quest of "pardon" clearly
recalls the Book of Common Prayer, the order of
religious worship in the England of Shakespeare's
day, where those who have "offended" are likewise
urged to make "amends". From this point of
view, "the serpent's tongue" that threatens the
actors suggests not only the hissing of a dissatisfied
theatre audience, but the sting of sin. But if we
approve of the play, the giving of our hands – in
applause, but also in an image of hand-clasping
fellowship – shows we still share community after
"all the story of the night told o'er". If the actors
have transgressed against power or comfort,
wittingly or otherwise, their offer of repentance
and amends ought to be acceptable. To refuse it

would put ourselves in turn outside charity.

Puck's speech also puts another spin on this offer. His version of "mending" invites the audience to regard the whole play as trivial: "no more yielding but a dream". But there is a real question of how much a dream can "yield". Given that the play has taken some pains to show that the "yielding" of a dream may be quite complex, Puck's attempt to reassure the audience by concealing any disturbing aspects under the comforting blanket of "just a dream" is a sly ruse. Puck, of course, does not care – call him a liar and you simply name the truth of his nature. He flies away regardless, "following darkness like a dream". Poets, too, have been called liars before, and have evaded the charge. As Sir Philip Sidney, Shakespeare's older contemporary, insisted : "For the poet, he nothing affirms, and therefore never lieth." The true yielding of dreams, as of poems or of plays, is not to be sought in terms of simple accuracy or falsity, but rather in depth and clarity of perception, richness of development, density of experience, resonance of image. So though Puck offers his apologies in good faith, he also reserves the right to tell us that, if we don't like the play, it may be because we have not yet understood it (just as Theseus has failed to understand the performance of "Pyramus and Thisbe"). Perhaps if we did, it would offend us even more deeply. Being a shadow is sometimes a complicated business.

What view of the world does *A Midsummer Night's Dream* leave us with?

I believe marriages would in general be as happy, and often more so, if they were all made by the Lord Chancellor, upon a due consideration of characters and circumstances, without the parties having any choice in the matter.

Boswell, *reporting the opinion of Dr Johnson*

Dr Johnson was what we would now call a realist; he speaks with a rational sobriety that sees erotic passion as an unreliable index to lasting happiness. Of course, he means to be provocative, though not frivolous or flippant. Sobriety has looked on passion and found it wanting. Dr Johnson's vision would maintain the interest of the state in settled circumstances by simply taking the power to make marriages away from the parties themselves and vesting it directly in the Lord Chancellor. He is a Theseus in his scepticism, if not in his marital history.

But Shakespeare is a poet and a playwright, not a social engineer. He is interested in the complexities, conflicts and contradictions that make up human lives. Among the most vexing of these is sexual passion, in which mastery and submission, longing and flight, self-possession and self-abandon circle around and through one another. In love, says his poetry, we are never ourselves, but always impelled beyond ourselves. And yet the reaching beyond which so often undoes us is also the heart – the undiscovered country – of our deepest imaginative energies, its

MUSIC IN THE PLAY

Music was among the pleasures Shakespeare's company offered its audiences, and the playhouse had professional musicians to provide it: fanfares, entries, songs, dances and so on. But Shakespeare's plays are especially interested in music as a form of complex human expression, and *A Midsummer Night's Dream* shares this interest.

The play contains many pieces of music and musical effects: the lullaby for the Fairy Queen, Bottom's song that awakens her, the reconciliation dance of Oberon and Titania, the horns that accompany Theseus and Hippolyta on the hunt, the "bergomask" folkdance at the end of "Pyramus and Thisbe", the bell with its "iron tongue" calling "lovers to bed", the final ceremonial dance of the fairies. Other music is mentioned but not heard: the songs Lysander sang under Hermia's window, the "sea-maid's music" Oberon witnessed, the musical hunting dogs, even Bottom's call for "the tongs and the bones" for Titania. The play's soundscape is rich with music both heard and unheard.

This music is not just decorative. It is a strong image of art-making, very contradictoriness defining its power.

In a short and powerful poem from later in his career, "The Phoenix and the Turtle", Shakespeare imagined a chorus of birds celebrating and lamenting the love of a strange couple – a phoenix and a turtledove – that passed into and fully lived out those contradictions:

---

a counterpart of the workaday manufacture of household objects by the "mechanicals". We can see this from the way Theseus discusses the sounds his dogs make on their hunting:

THESEUS:
     We will, fair queen, up to the mountain's top,
     And mark the musical confusion
     Of hounds and echo in conjunction.
HIPPOLYTA:
     I was with Hercules and Cadmus once,
     When in a wood of Crete they bayed the bear
     With hounds of Sparta: never did I hear
     Such gallant chiding: for, besides the groves,
     The skies, the fountains, every region near

     Seemed all one mutual cry: I never heard
     So musical a discord, such sweet thunder.

Theseus's dogs are also "match'd in mouth like bells,/ Each under each". This image of musical hounds shows Theseus arranging and appreciating sound, and it also recalls the patterning of incongruities that Shakespeare effects in his play, made up of such disparate elements, so that we may ask, as Theseus does later, "How shall we find the concord of this discord?" The play, like the dogs' barking, is a pleasing and harmonious design that contains and controls potentially dangerous energies – as indeed does the myth of Theseus himself ∎

So between them Love did shine,
That the Turtle saw his right,
Flaming in the Phoenix' sight;
Either was the other's mine.

Property was thus appalled,
That the self was not the same :
Single Nature's double name,
Neither two nor one was called.

Reason in itself confounded,
Saw Division grow together,
To themselves yet either neither,
Simple were so well compounded.

In this lament, or hymn, the language of understanding wears thin, its normal procedures – number, person, grammar – collapsing under the impact of love. But where Reason confounds, Poetry triumphs. So Helena, in more compact form, beholds her love for Demetrius upon waking in the wood – "Mine own and not mine own". Yet to live such paradox, to resolve such energies, is dangerous. The ecstatic birds of the poem burn up in passion for each other, and are not reborn. In the Athenian wood, the lovers very nearly come to grief. Bottom's Dream, the dream of the world unveiled to the imagination's eye, is finally unspeakable.

Shakespeare's *A Midsummer Night's Dream* is a masterpiece of balance and formal control, weaving together its various lines of story with so little apparent effort that their incongruities almost vanish. It was revolutionary in its time – the most complicated piece of plotting in a single play written in English. It is held tightly together by a series of intertwined themes – dreams, love, imagination, power – and by a lyrical energy at once enthralling and playful, blithe and self-conscious. It is deliberately, even extravagantly, an artefact, a piece of ingenuity that announces its poet's confident mastery.

At the same time, this glittering masterpiece gains its very particular intensity from harnessing energies that lead directly into darker corners of human life. Shakespeare's happy comedy, ending in three marriages, has a constant awareness of danger. Its view of us mortals is roughly Puck's, but without his happy unconcern: "Lord, what fools these mortals be!" We are fools because we cannot help being fools. But our folly is also a blessing: the paradox at the heart of *A Midsummer Night's Dream* is that the source of all that's best in the world is also the source of all that is most dangerous and destructive. The abrupt reversals and changes of behaviour we see in the wood reflect all this. They also, writes Harold Brooks, "raise doubts about the self-consistency, even the continuous existence, of personal identity, and whether we are not, in Auden's words, 'lived by powers we pretend to understand'." Brooks adds:

"They raise these doubts; they do not endorse them, as in an absurdist frame of mind a modern sceptic might." But one might argue that if the play doesn't "endorse" these doubts it certainly doesn't resolve or deny them.

G. Wilson Knight spoke of how Shakespeare's poetry gives the impression "less of a surface than of a turbulent power, a heave and swell, from deeps beyond verbal definition". Our consciousness, our daytime happiness, the little lives and histories upon which we lavish so much energy, are merely lifebelts sustaining us over thick deeps we may be better off not looking into. But art and dreams invite us to look, whether we want to or not.

Opposite: Michelle Pfeiffer as Titania in Michael Hoffman's 1999 film

A SHORT CHRONOLOGY

*c.*1300 BC Theseus supposed to have been born

43 BC Ovid born

Late 1380s Geoffrey Chaucer writes "The Knight's Tale" for *The Canterbury Tales*, one source for the Theseus/Hippolyta plot in the *Dream*.

1567 Ovid's *Metamorphoses*, another important source for the *Dream*, translated into English

1558 Elizabeth I comes to the throne

1564 Shakespeare born in Stratford-upon-Avon

1590 First instalment of Edmund Spenser's *The Faerie Queen*. Second instalment followed in 1596.

1594 *Love's Labour's Lost*

1595-96 Probable date of *A Midsummer Night's Dream*

1595-96 *Romeo and Juliet*

1600 Publication of the *Dream* in quarto (single-volume like a modern small paperback). A second quarto edition followed in 1619.

1601 Shakespeare's *The Phoenix and The Turtle* published

1603 Elizabeth 1 dies, accession of James I

1604 January 1 Performance at the court of King James of *A Play of Robin Goodfellow*, thought by some scholars to have been the *Dream* with a modified title for this performance.

1662 Restoration diarist Samuel Pepys calls *A Midsummer Night's Dream* "the most insipid, ridiculous play that I ever saw".

1827 Felix Mendelssohn composes music for a Prussian production. The music has been frequently used since on stage and in films.

1935 Max Reinhardt's lavish film production of the *Dream*, starring Olivia de Havilland, James Cagney and Mickey Rooney, and set to Mendelssohn's music.

1964 Jan Kott's *Shakespeare Our Contemporary*, with its emphasis on what he saw as the darkness and bestial sexuality of the *Dream*.

1970 Peter Brook's RSC production, using trapezes and set in a blank white box, doubles Theseus/Hippolyta with Oberon/Titania.

1999 Michael Hoffman sets the *Dream* in the Victorian era for his film starring Michele Pfeiffer, Rupert Everett, Christian Bale, Calista Flockhart and Kevin Kline.

BIBLIOGRAPHY

Barber, C.L., *Shakespeare's Festive Comedy* Princeton University Press, 1972

Bate, Jonathan, *Shakespeare and Ovid*, Clarendon, 1993

Bradshaw, Graham, *Shakespeare's Scepticism*, Harvester, 1987

Brooks, Harold ed., *A Midsummer Night's Dream* Arden Shakespeare, 1979

Calderwood, James, *A Midsummer Night's Dream* Harvester Wheatsheaf, 1992

Coleridge, Samuel, "Notes on the Comedies of Shakespeare…" repr. in *Shakespearean Criticism*, ed. Thomas Raysor, vol. 1, Dutton, 1960

Couliano, Ioan, *Eros and Magic in the Renaissance*, University of Chicago Press, 1987

Dutton, Richard ed., *New Casebooks: A Midsummer Night's Dream. Contemporary Critical Essays* Macmillan, 1996

Eagleton, Terry, William Shakespeare, Blackwell, 1986

Fender, Stephen, *A Midsummer Night's Dream,* Edward Arnold, 1968

Empson, William, "The Spirits of the 'Dream'" in Essays on Renaissance Literature, vol. 2, ed. John Haffenden, Cambridge University Press, 1994 Frye, Northrop, *A Natural Perspective: the Development of Shakesearean Comedy and Romance,* Columbia University Press, 1965

Garber, Marjorie B., *Dream in Shakespeare,* Yale University Press, 1974

Garner, Shirley Nelson, "*A Midsummer Night's Dream - 'Jack Shall Have Jill:/ Nought Shall Go Ill'"* in Kehler, Dorothea ed., *A Midsummer Night's Dream: Critical Essays,* New York: Garland Publishing, 1998

Hackett, Helen, "A Midsummer Night's Dream" in A Companion to Shakespeare's Works, Vol 3, Blackwell, 2003 Halio, Jay L., *A Midsummer Night's Dream – Shakespeare in Performance,* Manchester University Press,1994

Hendricks, Margo, "Obscured by dreams: Race, Empire, and Shakespeare's *A Midsummer Night's Dream*", *Shakespeare Quarterly* 47:1. (1996), pp. 37-60

Hinely, Jan, "Expounding the Dream…" in *Psychoanalytic Approaches to Literature and Film*, Fairleigh Dickinson University Press, 1987

Holland, Peter ed., *A Midsummer Night's Dream,* Oxford University Press, 1998

Holland, Norman, "Hermia's Dream", 1979 essay repr. *In Representing Shakespeare: New Psychoanalytic Essays*, Johns Hopkins University Press, 1980

Kehler, Dorothea ed., *A Midsummer Night's Dream: Critical Essays* Garland Publishing, 1998

Kermode, Frank, "The Mature Comedies" in *Early Shakespeare*, ed. John Russell Brown and Bernard Harris, Edward Arnold, 1961

Kott, Jan, *Shakespeare, our contemporary London*: Methuen, 1964

Marshall, David, "Exchanging Visions: Reading *A Midsummer Night's Dream*" in *English Literary History* 49:3 (1982), pp. 543-575

Montrose, Louis., *The purpose of playing : Shakespeare and the cultural politics of the Elizabethan theatre* Chicago University Press, 1996

Nuttall, A.D., *Shakespeare the Thinker*, Yale University Press, 2007

Olson, Paul, "A Midsummer Night's Dream and the Meaning of Court Marriage", ELH 24, 1957

Paglia, Camille, *Sexual Personae: Art and Decadence from Nefertiti to Emily Dickinson*, Yale University Press, 1990

Palfrey, Simon, *Doing Shakespeare*, Methuen, 2005

Parker, Patricia, *Shakespeare from the Margins: Language, Culture, Context*, University of Chicago Press, 1996

Pennington, Michael, *A Midsummer Night's Dream: A User's Guide,* Nick Hern Books: 2005

Selbourne, David, *The Making of* A Midsummer Night's Dream*, an eye-witness account of Peter Brook's production from first rehearsal to first night,* Methuen, 1982

Rougemont, Denis de, *Passion and Society*, Faber and Faber, 1956

Tave, Stuart, *Lovers, Clowns and Fairies: An Essay on Comedies*, University of Chicago Press, 1993

Tanner, Tony, introduction, *William Shakespeare: Comedies, Vol. 1*, Everyman, 1906

Williams, Gary Jay, *Our Moonlit Revels:* A Midsummer Night's Dream *in the Theatre*, University of Iowa Press, 1997

Yachnin, Paul, "The Politics of Theatrical Mirth: *A Midsummer Night's Dream,* A Mad World, My Masters, and *Measure for Measure*", *Shakespeare Quarterly* 43:1 (1992), pp. 51-66

Young, David, *Something of great constancy: the art of* A Midsummer Night's Dream, Yale University Press, 1966.

INDEX

First published in 2012 by
Connell Guides
Spye Arch House
Spye Park
Lacock
Chippenham
Wiltshire SN15 2PR

10 9 8 7 6 5 4 3 2 1

Picture credits:
p.15 © Express/ Archive Photos/ Getty Images
p.33 © Rex Features
p.45 © Bridgeman Art Library
p.49 © Getty Images
p.53 © Moviestore Collection/ Rex Features
p.57 © Alastair Muir/ Rex Features
p71 © AF Images/ Rex Features
p.81© Daily Mail/ Rex Features
p.85 © Moviestore Collection/ Rex Features
p.97 © Rex Features
p.105 © Associated Press/ Rex Features
p.119 © Corbis

A CIP catalogue record for this book is available from the British Library.
ISBN 978-1-907776-18-2

Assistant Editor: Katie Sanderson
Typesetting: Katrina ffiske
Design © Nathan Burton
Printed in Great Britain by Butler Tanner & Dennis

www.connellguides.com